Anna Letitia Barbauld

Devotional Pieces, Compiled from the Psalms and the Book of Job

To which are prefixed, thoughts on the devotional taste, on sects, and on

establishments

Anna Letitia Barbauld

Devotional Pieces, Compiled from the Psalms and the Book of Job
To which are prefixed, thoughts on the devotional taste, on sects, and on establishments

ISBN/EAN: 9783337043032

Printed in Europe, USA, Canada, Australia, Japan

Cover: Foto ©Lupo / pixelio.de

More available books at **www.hansebooks.com**

DEVOTIONAL PIECES,

COMPILED FROM THE

PSALMS

AND THE

BOOK OF JOB:

TO WHICH ARE PREFIXED,

THOUGHTS

ON THE

DEVOTIONAL TASTE,

ON SECTS, AND ON

ESTABLISHMENTS.

Praife is devotion fit for mighty minds;
The differing world's agreeing facrifice.
                              GONDIBERT.

LONDON:

PRINTED FOR J. JOHNSON, No. 72, ST. PAUL'S
CHURCH-YARD.

MDCCLXXV.

TO THE

Rev^D. JOHN AIKIN, D.D.

PROFESSOR OF DIVINITY

IN THE ACADEMY AT WARRINGTON;

THIS PIECE,

INTENDED TO SERVE THAT CAUSE,

TO WHICH THE LABOURS OF HIS LIFE

HAVE BEEN SO HONOURABLY AND SUCCESSFULLY DEVOTED;

THE CAUSE OF RELIGION AND VIRTUE;

AS A TESTIMONY OF VENERATION

FOR THE MOST RESPECTABLE OF CHARACTERS;

AS A TRIBUTE OF DUTY

TO THE TENDEREST OF PARENTS;

IS INSCRIBED,

BY HIS GRATEFUL AND OBEDIENT DAUGHTER,

PALGRAVE, SUFFOLK,
July 10th, 1775.   ANNA LÆTITIA BARBAULD.

CONTENTS.

THOUGHTS on the Devotional Taste, on Sects, and on Establishments. - - Page 1.

PART I.

Moral Psalms. - - 53.

PART II.

Psalms of Praise, Penitence, and Prayer. - - 79.

PART III.

Occasional and Prophetic Psalms. 171.

THOUGHTS

ON THE

DEVOTIONAL TASTE,

on SECTS,

and on

ESTABLISHMENTS.

THOUGHTS

ON THE

DEVOTIONAL TASTE,

on SECTS, and on

ESTABLISHMENTS.

IT is obferved by a late moſt amiable and elegant writer, that Religion may be confidered in three different views. As a ſyſtem of opinions, its ſole object is truth, and the only faculty that has any thing to do with it is Reaſon, exerted in the freeſt and moſt diſpaſſionate inquiry. As a principle regulating our conduct,

conduct, Religion is a habit, and like all other habits, of flow growth, and gaining strength only by repeated exertions. But it may likewise be considered as a taste, an affair of sentiment and feeling, and in this sense it is properly called Devotion. Its seat is in the imagination and the passions, and it has its source in that relish for the sublime, the vast, and the beautiful, by which we taste the charms of poetry and other compositions that address our finer feelings; rendered more lively and interesting by a sense of gratitude for personal benefits. It is in a great degree constitutional, and is by no means found in exact proportion to the virtue of a character.

It is with relation to this last view of the subject that the observations in this essay are hazarded: for though as a rule of life, the authority and salutary effects of of religion are pretty univerfally acknowledged, and though its tenets have been defended with fufficient zeal; its affections languifh, the fpirit of Devotion is certainly at a very low ebb amongft us, and what is furprifing, it has fallen, I know not how, into a certain contempt, and is treated with great indifference, amongft many of thofe who value themfelves on the purity of their faith, and who are diftinguifhed by the fweetnefs of their morals. As the religious affections in a great meafure rife and fall with the pulfe, and are affected by every thing which acts upon the imagination, they are apt to run into ftrange exceffes, and if directed by a melancholy or enthufiaftic faith, their workings are often too ftrong for a weak head, or a delicate frame; and for this reafon they have been almoft excluded from religious worfhip by many perfons of real piety. It is the character of the present age to allow little to sentiment, and all the warm and generous emotions are treated as romantic by the supercilious brow of a cold-hearted philosophy. The man of science, with an air of superiority, leaves them to some florid declaimer who professes to work upon the passions of the lower class, where they are so debased by noise and nonsense, that it is no wonder if they move disgust in those of elegant and better-informed minds.

Yet there is a devotion generous, liberal, and humane, the child of more exalted feelings than base minds can enter into, which assimilates man to higher natures, and lifts him "above this visible diurnal sphere." Its pleasures are ultimate, and when early cultivated continue vivid even in that uncomfortable season of life when some of the passions are extinct, when imagination is dead, and the heart begins

begins to contract within itself. Those who want this taste, want a sense, a part of their nature, and should not presume to judge of feelings to which they must ever be strangers. No one pretends to be a judge in poetry or the fine arts, who has not both a natural and a cultivated relish for them; and shall the narrow-minded children of earth absorbed in low pursuits, dare to treat as visionary, objects which they have never made themselves acquainted with? Silence on such subjects will better become them. But to vindicate the pleasures of devotion from those who have neither taste nor knowledge about them, is not the present object. It rather deserves our inquiry, what causes have contributed to check the operation of religious impressions amongst those who have steady principles, and are well disposed to virtue.

AND, in the first place, there is nothing more prejudicial to the feelings of a devout heart, than a habit of disputing on religious subjects. Free inquiry is undoubtedly necessary to establish a rational belief; but a disputatious spirit, and fondness for controversy, gives the mind a sceptical turn, with an aptness to call in question the most established truths. It is impossible to preserve that deep reverence for the Deity with which we ought to regard him, when all his attributes, and even his very existence become the subject of familiar debate. Candor demands that a man allow his opponent an unlimited freedom of speech, and it is not easy in the heat of discourse to avoid falling into an indecent or a careless expression; hence those who think seldomer of religious subjects, often treat them with more respect than those whose profession keeps them constantly in their view. A
sober

sober Officer would be shocked to hear questions of this nature treated with that ease and negligence with which they are generally discussed by the practised Theologian, or the young lively Academic ready primed from the schools of logic and metaphysics. In general, I believe we may venture to assert, that no man, who has a proper veneration for the primary truths of religion, will be fond of making them the subjects of common discourse; any more than a person who loved with ardour and delicacy would chuse to introduce the name of his mistress amongst mixed companies in every light and trivial conversation. The regard in both cases would be deep and silent, and not apt to vent itself in words, unless called forth by some interesting occasion. As the ear loses its delicacy by being only obliged to hear coarse and vulgar language, so the veneration for religion wears off by hearing it treated with difregard, though we ourfelves are employed in defending it; and to this it is owing that many who have confirmed themfelves in the belief of religion, have never been able to recover that ftrong and affectionate fenfe of it which they had before they began to inquire, and have wondered to find their devotion weaker when their faith was better grounded. Indeed, ftrong reafoning powers and quick feelings do not often unite in the fame perfon. Men of a fcientific turn feldom lay their hearts open to impreffion. Previoufly biaffed by the love of fyftem, they do indeed attend the offices of religion, but they dare not truft themfelves with the preacher, and are continually upon the watch to obferve whether every fentiment agrees with their own particular tenets.

The fpirit of inquiry is eafily diftinguifhed

guished from the spirit of disputation. A state of doubt is not a pleasant state. It is painful, anxious, and distressing beyond most others: it disposes the mind to dejection and modesty. Whoever therefore is so unfortunate as not to have settled his opinions in important points, will proceed in the search of truth with deep humility, unaffected earnestness, and a serious attention to every argument that may be offered, which he will be much rather inclined to revolve in his own mind, than to use as materials for dispute. Even with these dispositions, it is happy for a man when he does not find much to alter in the religious system he has embraced; for if that undergoes a total revolution, his religious feelings are too generally so weakened by the shock, that they hardly recover again their original tone and vigour.

SHALL

Shall we mention Philosophy as an enemy to Religion? God forbid! Philosophy,

> Daughter of Heaven, that flow ascending still
> Investigating sure the form of things
> With radiant finger points to heaven again.

Yet there is a view in which she exerts an influence perhaps rather unfavourable to the fervor of simple piety. Philosophy does indeed enlarge our conceptions of the Deity, and gives us the sublimest ideas of his power and extent of dominion; but it raises him too high for our imaginations to take hold of, and in a great measure destroys that affectionate regard which is felt by the common class of pious christians. When, after contemplating the numerous productions of this earth, the various forms of being, the laws, the mode of their existence, we rise yet higher, and turn our eyes to that magnifi-

magnificent profusion of suns and systems which astronomy pours upon the mind— When we grow acquainted with the majestic order of nature, and those eternal laws which bind the material and intellectual worlds— When we trace the footsteps of creative energy through regions of unmeasured space, and still find new wonders disclosed and pressing upon the view —we grow giddy with the prospect; the mind is astonished — confounded at its own insignificance; we think it almost impiety for a worm to lift its head from the dust, and address the Lord of so stupendous a universe; the idea of communion with our Maker seems shocking, and the only feeling the soul is capable of in such a moment is a deep and painful sense of its own abasement. It is true, the same philosophy teaches that the Deity is intimately present through every part of this complicated system, and neglects not any

of

of his works: but this is a truth which is believed without being felt; our imagination cannot here keep pace with reason, and the Sovereign of nature seems ever further removed from us in proportion as the bounds of the creation are enlarged.

PHILOSOPHY represents the Deity in too abstracted a manner to engage our affections. A Being without hatred and without fondness, going on in one steady course of even benevolence, neither delighted with praises, nor moved by importunity, does not interest us so much as a character open to the feelings of indignation, the soft relentings of mercy, and the partialities of particular affections. We require some common nature, or at least the appearance of it, on which to build our intercourse. It is also a fault of which philosophers are often guilty, that they dwell too much in generals.

Accuftomed to reduce every thing to the operation of general laws, they turn our attention to larger views, attempt to grafp the whole order of the univerfe, and in the zeal of a fyftematic fpirit feldom leave room for thofe particular and perfonal mercies which are the food of gratitude. They trace the great outline of nature, but neglect the colouring which gives warmth and beauty to the piece. As in poetry it is not vague and general defcription, but a few ftriking circumftances clearly related and ftrongly worked up — as in a landfcape it is not fuch a vaft extenfive range of country as pains the eye to ftretch to its limits, but a beautiful well-defined profpect, which gives the moft pleafure — fo neither are thofe unbounded views in which philofophy delights, fo much calculated to touch the heart as home views and nearer objects. The philofopher offers up general praifes on the

the altar of univerfal nature; the devout man, on the altar of his heart, prefents his own fighs, his own thankfgivings, his own earneft defires: the former worfhip is more grand, the latter more perfonal and affecting.

We are likewife too fcrupulous in our public exercifes, and too ftudious of accuracy. A prayer ftrictly philofophical muft ever be a cold and dry compofition. From an over-anxious fear of admitting any expreffion that is not ftrictly proper, we are apt to reject all warm and pathetic imagery, and in fhort, every thing that ftrikes upon the heart and the fenfes. But it may be faid, If the Deity be indeed fo fublime a being, and if his defigns and manner are fo infinitely beyond our comprehenfion, how can a thinking mind join in the addreffes of the vulgar, or avoid being overwhelmed with the indiftinct

vaftnefs

vastness of such an idea. Far be it from me to deny that awe and veneration must ever make a principal part of our regards to the Master of the universe, or to defend that stile of indecent familiarity which is yet more shocking than indifference: but let it be considered that we cannot hope to avoid all improprieties in speaking of such a Being; that the most philosophical address we can frame is probably no more free from them than the devotions of the vulgar; that the scriptures set us an example of accommodating the language of prayer to common conceptions, and making use of figures and modes of expression far from being strictly defensible; and that upon the whole it is safer to trust to our genuine feelings, feelings implanted in us by the God of nature, than to any metaphysical subtleties. He has impressed me with the idea of trust and confidence, and my heart flies to him in danger; of mercy to forgive, and I melt before him in penitence; of bounty to bestow, and I ask of him all I want or wish for. I may make use of an inaccurate expression, I may paint him to my imagination too much in the fashion of humanity; but while my heart is pure, while I depart not from the line of moral duty, the error is not dangerous. Too critical a spirit is the bane of every thing great or pathetic. In our creeds let us be guarded, let us there weigh every syllable; but in compositions addressed to the heart, let us give freer scope to the language of the affections, and the overflowing of a warm and generous disposition.

Another cause which most effectually operates to check devotion, is Ridicule. I speak not here of open derision of things sacred; but there is a certain ludicrous style

style in talking of such subjects, which without any ill design does much harm: and perhaps those whose studies or profession lead them to be chiefly conversant with the offices of religion, are most apt to fall into this impropriety; for their ideas being chiefly taken from that source, their common conversation is apt to be tinctured with fanciful allusions to scripture expressions, to prayers, &c. which have all the effect of a parody, and like parodies, destroy the force of the finest passage, by associating it with something trivial and ridiculous. Of this nature is Swift's well-known jest of "Dearly beloved Roger," which whoever has strong upon his memory, will find it impossible to attend with proper seriousness to that part of the service. We should take great care to keep clear from all these trivial associations, in whatever we wish to be regarded as venerable.

Another species of ridicule to be avoided, is that kind of sneer often thrown upon those whose hearts are giving way to honest emotion. There is an extreme delicacy in all the finer affections, which makes them shy of observation, and easily checked. Love, Wonder, Pity, the enthusiasm of Poetry, shrink from the notice of even an indifferent eye, and never indulge themselves freely but in solitude, or when heightened by the powerful force of sympathy. Observe an ingenuous youth at a well-wrought tragedy. If all around him are moved, he suffers his tears to flow freely; but if a single eye meets him with a glance of contemptuous indifference, he can no longer enjoy his sorrow, he blushes at having wept, and in a moment his heart is shut up to every impression of tenderness. It is sometimes mentioned as a reproach to Protestants, that they are susceptible of a false shame when observed

in

in the exercises of their religion, from which Papists are free. But I take this to proceed from the purer nature of our religion; for the less it is made to consist in outward pomp and mechanical worship, and the more it has to do with the finer affections of the heart, the greater will be the reserve and delicacy which attends the expression of its sentiments. Indeed, ridicule ought to be very sparingly used, for it is an enemy to every thing sublime or tender: the least degree of it, whether well or ill founded, suddenly and instantaneously stops the workings of passion; and those who indulge a talent that way, would do well to consider, that they are rendering themselves for ever incapable of all the higher pleasures either of taste or morals. More especially do these cold pleasantries hurt the minds of youth, by checking that generous expansion of heart to which their open tempers are naturally

prone,

prone, and producing a vicious shame, through which they are deprived of the enjoyment of heroic sentiments or generous action.

In the next place, let us not be superstitiously afraid of superstition. It shews great ignorance of the human heart, and the springs by which its passions are moved, to neglect taking advantage of the impression which particular circumstances, times and seasons, naturally make upon the mind. The root of all superstition is the principle of the association of ideas, by which, objects naturally indifferent become dear and venerable, through their connection with interesting ones. It is true, this principle has been much abused: it has given rise to pilgrimages innumerable, worship of relics, and priestly power. But let us not carry our ideas of purity and simplicity so far, as to neglect it entirely.

tirely. Superior natures, it is poffible, may be equally affected with the fame truths at all times, and in all places; but we are not fo made. Half the pleafures of elegant minds are derived from this fource. Even the enjoyments of fenfe without it would lofe much of their attraction. Who does not enter into the fentiment of the Poet, in that paffage fo full of nature and truth:

' He that outlives this hour and comes fafe home,
' Shall ftand on tiptoe when this day is named,
' And roufe him at the name of Crifpian:
' He that outlives this day and fees old age,
' Will yearly on the vigil feaft his neighbours,
' And fay, To morrow is St. Crifpian.'

But were not the benefits of the victory equally apparent on any other day of the year? Why commemorate the anniverfary with fuch diftinguifhed regard? Thofe who can afk fuch a queftion, have never attended to some of the strongest instincts in our nature. Yet it has lately been the fashion, amongst those who call themselves rational christians, to treat as puerile, all attentions of this nature when relative to religion. They would

> Kiss with pious lips the sacred earth
> Which gave a Hampden or a Russel birth.

They will visit the banks of Avon with all the devotion of enthusiastic zeal; celebrate the birth-day of the hero and the patriot; and yet pour contempt upon the man who suffers himself to be warmed by similar circumstances relating to his Master, or the connection of sentiments of peculiar reverence with times, places, and men which have been appropriated to the service of religion. A wise preacher will not, from a fastidious refinement, disdain to affect his hearers from the season of the year, the anniversary of a national blessing, a remarkable escape from danger,

or

DEVOTIONAL TASTE, &c. 23

or, in short, any incident that is sufficiently guarded, and far enough removed from what is trivial, to be out of danger of becoming ludicrous.

It will not be amiss to mention here, a reproach which has been cast upon devotional writers, that they are apt to run into the language of love. Perhaps the charge would be full as just, had they said that Love borrows the language of Devotion; for the votaries of that passion are fond of using those exaggerated expressions, which can suit nothing below divinity; and you can hardly address the greatest of all Beings in a strain of more profound adoration, than the lover uses to the object of his attachment. But the truth is, Devotion does in no small degree resemble that fanciful and elevated kind of love which depends not on the senses. Nor is the likeness to be wondered at,

since

since both have their source in the love of beauty and excellence. Both are exceeding prone to superstition, and apt to run into romantic excesses. Both are nourished by poetry and music, and felt with the greatest fervour in the warmer climates. Both carry the mind out of itself, and powerfully refine the affections from every thing grofs, low, and selfish.

But it is time to retire; we are treading upon enchanted ground, and shall be suspected by many of travelling towards the regions of chivalry and old romance. And were it so, many a fair majestic idea might be gathered from those forgotten walks, which would well answer the trouble of transplanting. It must however be owned, that very improper language has formerly been used on these subjects; but there cannot be any great danger of such excesses, where the mind is guarded by by a rational faith, and the social affections have full scope in the free commerce of society.

HAVING thus considered the various causes which contribute to deaden the feelings of devotion, it may not be foreign to the subject to inquire in what manner they are affected by the different modes of religion. I speak not of opinions; for these have much less influence upon the heart, than the circumstances which attend particular persuasions. A sect may only differ from an establishment, as one absurd opinion differs from another: but there is a character and cast of manners belonging to each, which will be perfectly distinct; and of a sect, the character will vary as it is a rising or a declining sect, persecuted or at ease. Yet while divines have wearied the world with canvassing contrary doctrines and jarring articles

ticles of faith, the philosopher has not considered as the subject deserved what situation was most favourable to virtue, sentiment, and pure manners. To a philosophic eye, free from prejudice, and accustomed to large views of the great polity carried on in the moral world, perhaps varying and opposite forms may appear proper, and well calculated for their respective ends; and he will neither wish entirely to destroy the old, nor wholly to crush the new.

The great line of division between different modes of religion, is formed by Establishments and Sects. In an infant sect, which is always in some degree a persecuted one, the strong union and entire affection of its followers, the sacrifices they make to principle, the force of novelty, and the amazing power of sympathy, all contribute to cherish devotion.

It

It rises even to passion, and absorbs every other sentiment. Severity of manners imposes respect; and the earnestness of the new proselytes renders them insensible to injury, or even to ridicule. A strain of eloquence, often coarse indeed, but strong and persuasive, works like leaven in the heart of the people. In this state, all outward helps are superfluous, the living spirit of devotion is amongst them, the world sinks away to nothing before it, and every object but one is annihilated. The social principle mixes with the flame, and renders it more intense; strong parties are formed, and friends or lovers are not more closely connected than the members of these little communities.

It is this kind of devotion, a devotion which those of more settled and peaceable times can only guess at, which made a-mends to the first Christians for all they resigned,

resigned, and all they suffered: this draws the martyr to a willing death, and enables the confessor to endure a voluntary poverty. But this stage cannot last long; the heat of persecution abates, and the fervour of zeal feels a proportionable decay. Now comes on the period of reasoning and examination. The principles which have produced such mighty effects on the minds of men, acquire an importance, and become objects of the public attention. Opinions are canvassed. Those who before bore testimony to their religion only by patient suffering, now defend it with argument; and all the keenness of polemical disquisition is awakened on either side. The fair and generous idea of religious liberty, which never originates in the breast of a triumphant party, now begins to unfold itself. To vindicate these rights, and explain these principles, learning, which in the former state was
despised,

despised, is assiduously cultivated by the
sectaries; their minds become enlightened, and a large portion of knowledge,
especially religious knowledge, is diffused
through their whole body. Their manners are less austere, without having as
yet lost any thing of their original purity.
Their ministers gain respect as writers,
and their pulpit discourses are studied and
judicious. The most unfavourable circumstance of this era is, that those who
dissent, are very apt to acquire a critical
and disputatious spirit; for, being continually called upon to defend doctrines in
which they differ from the generality,
their attention is early turned to the argu-
mentative part of religion; and hence we
see that sermons, which afford food for
this taste, are with them thought of more
importance than prayer and praise, though
these latter are undoubtedly the more genuine and indispensible parts of devotion.

THIS

This then is the second period; the third approaches fast: men grow tired of a controversy which becomes insipid from being exhausted; persecution has not only ceased, it begins to be forgotten; and from the absence of opposition in either kind, springs a fatal and spiritless indifference. That sobriety, industry, and abstinence from fashionable pleasures, which distinguished the fathers, has made the sons wealthy; and eager to enjoy their riches, they long to mix with that world, a separation from which was the best guard to their virtues. A secret shame creeps in upon them, when they acknowledge their relation to a disesteemed sect; they therefore endeavour to file off its peculiarities, but in so doing they destroy its very being. Connections with the establishment, whether of intimacy, business, or relationship, which formerly, from their superior zeal, turned to the advantage

tage of the sect, now operate against it. Yet these connections are formed more frequently than ever; and those who a little before, soured by the memory of recent suffering, betrayed perhaps an aversion from having any thing in common with the Church, now affect to come as near it as possible; and, like a little boat that takes a large vessel in tow, the sure consequence is, the being drawn into its vortex. They aim at elegance and show in their places of worship, the appearance of their preachers, &c. and thus impoliticly awaken a taste it is impossible they should ever gratify. They have worn off many forbidding singularities, and are grown more amiable and pleasing. But those singularities were of use: they set a mark upon them, they pointed them out to the world, and so obliged persons thus distinguished to exemplary strictness. No longer obnoxious to the world, they

are

are open to all the seductions of it. Their minister, that respectable character which once inspired reverence and affectionate esteem, their teacher and their guide, is now dwindled into the mere leader of the public devotions; or lower yet, a person hired to entertain them every week with an elegant discourse. In proportion as his importance decreases, his salary sits heavy on the people; and he feels himself depressed, by that most cruel of all mortifications to a generous mind, the consciousness of being a burden upon those from whom he derives his scanty support. Unhappily, amidst this change of manners, there are forms of strictness, and a set of phrases introduced in their first enthusiasm, which still subsist: these they are ashamed to use, and know not how to decline; and their behaviour, in consequence of them, is aukward and irresolute. Those who have

set

set out with the largest share of mysticism and flighty zeal, find themselves particularly embarrassed by this circumstance.

WHEN things are come to this crisis, their tendency is evident: and though the interest and name of a sect may be kept up for a time by the generosity of former ages, the abilities of particular men, or that reluctance which keeps a generous mind from breaking old connections; it must in a short course of years melt away into the establishment, the womb and the grave of all other modes of religion.

AN Establishment affects the mind by splendid buildings, music, the mysterious pomp of antient ceremonies; by the sacredness of peculiar orders, habits, and titles; by its secular importance; and by connecting with religion, ideas of order, dignity, and antiquity. It speaks to the heart,

heart, through the imagination and the senses; and though it never can raise devotion so high as we have described it in a beginning sect, it will preserve it from ever sinking into contempt. As to a woman in the glow of health and beauty, the most careless dress is the most becoming; but when the freshness of youth is worn off, greater attention is necessary, and rich ornaments are required to throw an air of dignity round her person: so while a sect retains its first plainness, simplicity, and affectionate zeal, it wants nothing an establishment could give; but that once declined, the latter becomes far more respectable. The faults of an establishment grow venerable from length of time; the improvements of a sect appear whimsical from their novelty. Antient families, fond of rank, and of that order which secures it to them, are on the side of the former. Traders incline to the latter;

latter; and so do generally men of genius, as it favours their originality of thinking. An establishment leans to superstition, a sect to enthusiasm; the one is a more dangerous and violent excess, the other more fatally debilitates the powers of the mind; the one is a deeper colouring, the other a more lasting dye: but the coldness and languor of a declining sect produces scepticism. Indeed, a sect is never stationary, as it depends entirely on passions and opinions; though it often attains excellence, it never rests in it, but is always in danger of one extreme or the other: whereas an old establishment, whatever else it may want, possesses the grandeur arising from stability.

We learn to respect whatever respects itself; and are easily led to think that system requires no alteration, which never admits of any. It is this circumstance, more than any other, which gives a dignity to that accumulated mafs of error, the Church of Rome. A fabric which has weathered many fucceffive ages, though the architecture be rude, the parts difproportionate, and overloaded with ornament, ftrikes us with a fort of admiration, merely from its having held fo long together.

The minifter of a fect, and of an eftablifhment, is upon a very different footing. The former is like the popular leader of an army; he is obeyed with enthufiafm while he is obeyed at all; but his influence depends on opinion, and is entirely perfonal: the latter refembles a general appointed by the monarch; he has foldiers lefs warmly devoted to him, but more fteady, and better difciplined. The diffenting teacher is nothing, if he have not the fpirit of a martyr; and is

the

the scorn of the world, if he be not above the world. The clergyman, possessed of power and affluence, and for that reason chosen from among the better ranks of people, is respected as a gentleman, though not venerated as an apostle; and as his profession generally obliges him to decent manners, his order is considered as a more regular and civilized class of men than their fellow-subjects of the same rank. The dissenting teacher, separated from the people, but not raised above them, invested with no power, entitled to no emoluments, if he cannot acquire for himself authority, must feel the bitterness of dependance. The ministers of the former denomination cannot fall, but in some violent convulsion of the state: those of the latter, when indifference and mutual neglect begin to succeed to that close union which once subsisted between them and their followers, lose their former influence

fluence without resource; the dignity and weight of their office is gone for ever, they feel the insignificancy of their pretensions, their spirits sink, and, except they take refuge in some collateral pursuit, and push for literary fame, they quickly degenerate into mere triflers. Their time is sacrificed to the most idle and frivolous compliances; their manners are effeminate, without being elegant: the world does not acknowledge them, for they are not of the world; it cannot esteem them, for they are not superior to the world.

Upon the whole, then, it should seem, that the strictness of a sect (and it can only be respectable by being strict) is calculated for a few finer spirits, who make Religion their chief object. As to the much larger number, on whom she has only an imperfect influence, making them decent

decent if not virtuous, and meliorating the heart without greatly changing it, for all thefe the genius of an eftablifhment is more eligible, and better fitted to cherifh that moderate devotion of which alone they are capable. All thofe who have not ftrength of mind to think for themfelves, who would live to virtue without denying the world, who wifh much to be religious, but more to be genteel—naturally flow into the eftablifhment. If it offered no motives to their minds, but fuch as are perfectly pure and fpiritual, their devotion would not for that be more exalted, it would die away to nothing; and it is better their minds fhould receive only a tincture of religion, than be wholly without it. Thofe too, whofe paffions are regular and equable, and who do not aim at abftracted virtues, are commonly placed to moft advantage within the pale of the national faith.

All the greater exertions of the mind, spirit to reform, fortitude and conſtancy to ſuffer, can be expected only from thoſe who, forſaking the common road, are exerciſed in a peculiar courſe of moral diſcipline: but it ſhould be remembered, that theſe exertions cannot be expected from every character, nor on every occaſion. Indeed, religion is a ſentiment which takes ſuch ſtrong hold on all the moſt powerful principles of our nature, that it may eaſily be carried to exceſs. The Deity never meant our regards to him ſhould engroſs the mind: that indifference to ſenſible objects, which many moraliſts preach, is not perhaps deſireable, except where the mind is raiſed above its natural tone, and extraordinary ſituations call forth extraordinary virtues.

If the peculiar advantages of a ſect were well underſtood, its followers would not be impatient of thoſe moderate reſtraints

ſtraints which do not riſe to perſecution, nor affect any of their more material intereſts: for, do they not bind them cloſer to each other, cheriſh zeal, and keep up the love of liberty? What is the language of ſuch reſtraints? Do they not ſay, with a prevailing voice, Let the timorous and the worldly depart; no one ſhall be of this perſuaſion, who is not ſincere, diſintereſted, conſcientious. It is notwithſtanding proper, that men ſhould be ſenſible of all their rights, aſſert them boldly, and proteſt againſt every infringement; for it may be of advantage to bear what yet it is unjuſtifiable in others to inflict.

Neither would diſſenters, if they attended to their real intereſts, be ſo ambitious as they generally are of rich converts. Such converts only accelerate their decline; they relax their diſcipline, and they

they acquire an influence very pernicious in societies which ought to breathe nothing but the spirit of equality.

SECTS are always strict, in proportion to the corruption of establishments, and the licentiousness of the times; and they are useful in the same proportion. Thus the austere lives of the primitive Christians counterbalanced the vices of that abandoned period; and thus the Puritans in the reign of Charles the Second seasoned with a wholesome severity the profligacy of public manners. They were less amiable than their descendants of the present day; but to be amiable was not the object: they were of public utility; and their scrupulous sanctity (carried to excess, themselves only considered) like a powerful antiseptic, opposed the contagion breathed from a most dissolute court. In like manner, that sect, one of whose most

moſt ſtriking characteriſtics is a beautiful ſimplicity of dialect, ſerved to check that ſtrain of ſervile flattery and Gothic compliment ſo prevalent in the ſame period, and to keep up ſome idea of that manly plainneſs with which one human being ought to addreſs another.

Thus have we ſeen that different modes of religion, though they bear little good-will to each other, are neverthelefs mutually uſeful. Perhaps there is not an eſtabliſhment ſo corrupt, as not to make the groſs of mankind better than they would be without it. Perhaps there is not a ſect ſo eccentric, but that it has ſet ſome one truth in the ſtrongeſt light, or carried ſome one virtue, before neglected, to its utmoſt height, or looſened ſome obſtinate and long-rooted prejudice. They anſwer their end; they die away; others ſpring up, and take their place. So the purer

part

part of the element, continually drawn off from the mighty mafs of waters, forms rivers, which running in various directions, fertilize large countries; yet, always tending towards the ocean, every acceffion to their bulk or grandeur but precipitates their courfe, and haftens their re-union with the common refervoir from which they were feparated.

In the mean time, the devout heart always finds affociates fuitable to its difpofition, and the particular caft of its virtues; while the continual flux and reflux of opinions prevents the active principles from ftagnating. There is an analogy between things material and immaterial. As from fome late experiments in philofophy it has been found, that the procefs of vegetation reftores and purifies vitiated air; fo does that moral and political ferment which accommpanies the growth of

new

new sects, communicate a kind of spirit and elasticity necessary to the vigour and health of the soul, but soon lost amidst the corrupted breath of an indiscriminate multitude.

IT remains now to say something of the following compilation. Unconnected as it seems with the preceding observations, the same turn of thought led to both. It was impossible to treat of the devotional spirit, without calling to mind the most beautiful compositions which that spirit ever inspired, the Psalms of David. In these, the boldest figures of the high Eastern poetry are united with a simplicity which makes them intelligible to the common ear. The sublimest ideas are given of the Deity; he is spoken of with the deepest reverence, and yet with all the warmth and pathos of personal gratitude and affection. Such pieces are certainly
proper

proper not only to be read as compositions, but to be used as acts of devotion, either in private, or in public and social worship. But unhappily, the very great mixture there is in these divine odes, renders them unfit for either of these purposes. We cannot enter into all the situations, and it would not be safe to adopt all the sentiments of their author; for the royal Poet had strong passions, and was very sensible to resentment, as well as to gratitude. Nor is this inconvenience sufficiently obviated by using only chosen pieces; for it is not easy, on the sudden, to make a selection: and besides, there are in the finest psalms exceptionable passages, and in the most improper ones some verses too beautiful to be lost.

It was hoped, therefore, that it might be of service to the cause of religion, to make a collection of the kind now offered to to the public. In this collection, all the Psalms which would bear it are given entire; others, where the connected sense could be preserved with such an omission, have only the exceptionable parts left out; and a third class is formed of separate passages scattered through several pieces, which are attempted to be formed into regular and distinct odes. With regard to their subjects, they may be divided into Moral, Devotional, and Occasional. Amongst the Occasional ones, but few have been admitted. The Devotional may be subdivided into Psalms of Praise, Penitence, and Prayer. Most of the Prophetic pieces are excluded, as not properly entering into the idea of worship. The book of Job, being so similar in style, has been taken into the scheme.

Some persons may perhaps expect, that in a plan like this, every phrase should

should be struck out that bore an allusion to the customs and worship of the Jews, or which contained idioms that in their literal sense we can no longer use. But this has not been thought necessary. These phrases are familiarized to the ear, and well understood by all Christians, who easily adapt them to their own ideas. Scripture expressions, and allusions to the scriptures, produce the same pleasing effect in a devotional piece, which allusions to the Greek and Roman authors do in a common poem; they form indeed the true classical style of these writings. The courts of Zion, and the walls of Jerusalem, are not more foreign to an English reader, than the hill of Parnassus, or the fountain of Hippocrene; and it ought to be no more an objection to a religious ode, that we are called upon to praise God with the psaltery and timbrel, than it is to a pastoral writer that he sings to

his

his pipe and his lyre, since both are equally diffused. Poetry cannot subsist without ornament; these are the appropriated ornaments of religious poetry, and contribute to give a picturesque air to compositions in which every other species of embellishment would be improper and unbecoming.

After all, it is not reading alone these noble pieces that will give us their full force: they must be really used as acts of worship. It was not in so cold, so unaffecting a manner, that the Psalms of David were first exhibited. The living voice of the people, the animating accompanyments of music, the solemnity of public pomp, the reverent prostrations of deep humility, or the exulting movements of pious joy, all conspired to raise, to touch, to subdue the heart. Perhaps a time may come, when our worship (amongst thofe at leaſt who are happy enough to be at liberty to make alterations) ſhall be new modelled by ſome free and enlarged genius. Perhaps the time may come, when the ſpirit of philoſophy, and the ſpirit of devotion, ſhall join to conduct our public aſſemblies; when to all that is graceful in order and well-regulated pomp, we ſhall add whatever is affecting in the warmth of zeal, and all that is delightful in the beauty of holineſs.

DEVOTIONAL PIECES,

COMPILED FROM THE

PSALMS

AND THE

BOOK OF JOB.

DEVOTIONAL PIECES.

PART I.

MORAL PSALMS.

I.

BLESSED is the man who walketh not in the counfel of the ungodly, nor ftandeth in the way of finners, nor fitteth in the feat of the fcornful.

But his delight is in the law of the Lord, and in his law doth he meditate day and night.

He fhall be like a tree planted by the rivers of water, that bringeth forth its fruit in its feafon.

evil, to cut off the remembrance of them from the earth.

The righteous cry, and the Lord heareth, and delivereth them out of all their troubles.

The Lord is nigh unto them that are of a broken heart, and saveth such as be of a contrite spirit.

Many are the afflictions of the righteous; but the Lord delivereth him out of them all.

He keepeth all his bones; not one of them is broken.

Evil shall slay the wicked; and they that hate the righteous shall be desolate.

The Lord redeemeth the soul of his servants; and none of them that trust in him shall be desolate.

IV.

FRET not thyself because of evil-doers, neither be thou envious against the workers of iniquity.

For they shall soon be cut down like the grass, and wither as the green herb.

Trust in the Lord, and do good; so shalt thou dwell in the land, and verily thou shalt be fed.

Delight

Delight thyself also in the Lord; and he shall give thee the desires of thine heart.

Commit thy way unto the Lord: trust also in him; and he shall bring it to pass.

And he shall bring forth thy righteousness as the light, and thy judgment as the noon-day.

Rest in the Lord, and wait patiently for him: fret not thyself because of him who prospereth in his way, because of the man who bringeth wicked devices to pass.

Cease from anger, and forsake wrath: fret not thyself in any wise to do evil.

For evil-doers shall be cut off: but those that wait upon the Lord, they shall inherit the earth.

For yet a little while and the wicked shall not be: yea, thou shalt diligently consider his place, and it shall not be.

But the meek shall inherit the earth; and shall delight themselves in the abundance of peace.

The wicked plotteth against the just, and gnasheth upon him with his teeth.

The Lord shall laugh at him: for he seeth that his day is coming.

The wicked have drawn out the sword, and have bent the bow, to cast down the poor and needy, and to slay such as be of upright conversation.

Their sword shall enter into their own heart, and their bows shall be broken.

A little that a righteous man hath, is better than the riches of many wicked.

For the arm of the wicked shall be broken: but the Lord upholdeth the righteous.

The Lord knoweth the days of the upright: and their inheritance shall be for ever.

They shall not be ashamed in the evil time: and in the days of famine they shall be satisfied.

But the wicked shall perish, and the enemies of the Lord shall be as the fat of lambs: they shall consume; into smoke shall they consume away.

The wicked borroweth, and payeth not again: but the righteous sheweth mercy, and giveth.

For such as be blessed of him shall inherit the earth; and they that be cursed of him shall be cut off.

The steps of the good man are ordered by the Lord: and he delighteth in his way.

Though he fall, he shall not be utterly cast down: for the Lord upholdeth him with his hand.

I have been young, and now am old; yet have I not seen the righteous forsaken, nor his seed begging bread.

He is ever merciful, and lendeth; and his seed is blessed.

Depart

Depart from evil, and do good; and dwell for evermore.

For the Lord loveth judgment, and forsaketh not his saints; they are preserved for ever: but the seed of the wicked shall be cut off.

The righteous shall inherit the land, and dwell therein for ever.

The mouth of the righteous speaketh wisdom, and his tongue talketh of judgment.

The law of his God is in his heart; none of his steps shall slide.

The wicked watcheth the righteous, and seeketh to slay him.

The Lord will not leave him in his hand, nor condemn him when he is judged.

I have seen the wicked in great power, and spreading himself like a green bay-tree.

Yet he passed away, and lo, he was not: yea, I sought him, but he could not be found.

Mark the perfect man, and behold the upright: for the end of that man is peace.

But the transgressors shall be destroyed together: the end of the wicked shall be cut off.

But the salvation of the righteous is of the Lord: he is their strength in the time of trouble.

And the Lord shall help them, and deliver them:

them: he shall deliver them from the wicked, and save them because they trust in him.

V.

HEAR this, all ye people; give ear, all ye inhabitants of the world:

Both low and high, rich and poor together.

My mouth shall speak of wisdom; and the meditation of my heart shall be of understanding.

They that trust in their wealth, and boast themselves in the multitude of their riches;

None of them can by any means redeem his brother, nor give to God a ransom for him:

That he should still live for ever, and not see corruption:

For the redemption of the soul is precious, and they are perished for ever.

Wise men die, likewise the fool and the brutish person perish, and leave their wealth to others.

Their inward thought is, that their houses shall continue for ever, and their dwelling-places to all generations: they call their lands after their own names.

Nevertheless, man being in honour, abideth not: he is like the beasts that perish.

This

This their way is their folly : yet their posterity approve their sayings.

Like sheep they are laid in the grave; death shall feed on them; and the upright shall have dominion over them in the morning; and their beauty shall consume in the grave, from their dwelling.

But God will redeem my soul from the power of the grave : for he shall receive me.

Be not thou afraid when one is made rich, when the glory of his house is increased.

For when he dieth, he shall carry nothing away : his glory shall not descend after him.

Though whilst he lived, he indulged his soul (and men will praise thee, when thou doest well to thyself)

He shall go to the generation of his fathers, he shall never see light.

Man that is in honour, abideth not, he is like the beasts that perish.

VI.

THE mighty God, even the Lord hath spoken, and called the earth even from the rising of the sun unto the going down thereof.

Out of Zion the perfection of beauty God hath shined.

Our God shall come, and shall not keep silence: a fire shall devour before him, and it shall be very tempestuous round about him.

He shall call to the heavens from above, and to the earth, that he may judge his people.

Gather my saints together unto me; those that have made a covenant with me by sacrifice.

And the heavens shall declare his righteousness: for God is judge himself.

Hear, O my people, and I will speak; O Israel, and I will testify against thee: I am God, even thy God.

I will not reprove thee for thy sacrifices, or thy burnt offerings; these have been continually before me.

I will take no bullock out of thy house, nor he-goat out of thy folds.

For every beast of the forest is mine, and the cattle upon a thousand hills.

I know all the fowls of the mountains: and the wild beasts of the field are mine.

If I were hungry, I would not tell thee: for the world is mine, and the fulness thereof.

Will I eat the flesh of bulls, or drink the blood of goats?

Offer unto God thankfgiving; and pay thy vows unto the moft High:

And call upon me in the day of trouble: I will deliver thee, and thou fhalt glorify me.

But unto the wicked God faith, what haft thou to do to declare my ftatutes, or that thou fhouldeft take my covenant into thy mouth?

Seeing thou hateft inftruction, and cafteft my words behind thee.

When thou faweft a thief, then thou confentedft with him, and haft been partaker with adulterers.

Thou giveft thy mouth to evil, and thy tongue frameth deceit.

Thou fitteft, and fpeakeft againft thy brother; thou flandereft thine own mother's fon.

Thefe things haft thou done, and I kept filence: thou thoughteft that I was altogether fuch an one as thyfelf: but I will reprove thee, and fet them in order before thine eyes.

Now confider this, ye that forget God, left he tear you in pieces, and there be none to deliver.

Whofo offereth praife, glorifieth me: and to him that ordereth his converfation aright will I fhew the falvation of God.

VII.

BLESSED is the man that feareth the Lord, that delighteth greatly in his commandments.

His feed fhall be mighty upon earth: the generation of the upright fhall be bleffed.

Wealth and riches fhall be in his houfe: and his righteoufnefs endureth for ever.

Unto the upright there arifeth light in the darknefs: he is gracious, and full of compaffion, and righteoufnefs.

A good man fheweth favour, and lendeth: he will guide his affairs with difcretion.

Surely he fhall not be moved for ever: the righteous fhall be had in everlafting remembrance.

He fhall not be afraid of evil tidings: his heart is fixed, trufting in the Lord.

His heart is eftablifhed, he fhall not be afraid.

He hath difperfed, he hath given to the poor; his righteoufnefs endureth for ever; his horn fhall be exalted with honour.

The wicked fhall fee it, and be grieved; he fhall gnafh with his teeth, and melt away: the defire of the wicked fhall perifh.

VIII.

VIII.

THEY that trust in the Lord shall be as mount Zion, which cannot be removed, but abideth for ever.

For the rod of the wicked shall not rest upon the lot of the righteous; lest the righteous put forth their hands unto iniquity.

Do good, O Lord, unto those that be good, and to them that are upright in their hearts.

As for such as turn aside unto their crooked ways, the Lord shall lead them forth with the workers of iniquity: but peace shall be upon his people.

IX.

BLESSED is every one that feareth the Lord; that walketh in his ways.

For thou shall eat the labour of thine hands: happy shall thou be, and it shall be well with thee.

Thy wife shall be as a fruitful vine by the side of thine house: thy children like olive plants round about thy table.

Behold, thus shall the man be blessed that feareth the Lord.

Yea,

Yea, thou shalt see thy children's children, and peace upon the land of thy habitation.

X.

BLESSED is he that confidereth the poor: the Lord shall deliver him in time of trouble.

The Lord will preserve him, and keep him alive; and he shall be blessed upon the earth: and thou wilt not deliver him unto the will of his enemies.

The Lord will strengthen him upon the bed of languishing: thou wilt smooth all his couch in his sickness.

A father of the fatherless, and a judge of the widows, is God in his holy habitation.

God setteth the solitary in families: he bringeth out those who are bound in chains; but the rebellious dwell in a dry land.

He will regard the prayer of the destitute, and not despise their prayer.

For he hath looked down from the height of his sanctuary: from heaven did the Lord behold the earth.

To hear the groaning of the prisoner, to loose those who are appointed unto death.

I will

I will greatly praife the Lord with my mouth; yea, I will praife him among the multitude.

For he fhall ftand at the right hand of the poor, to fave him from thofe who overwhelm his foul.

He that hath fet his love upon the Lord, the Lord will deliver him; he will fet him on high, becaufe he hath known his name.

He fhall call, and the Lord fhall anfwer: he will be with him in trouble; he will deliver him, and honour him.

With long life will he fatisfy him, and fhew him his falvation.

XI.

CAN man by fearching find out God? Can he find out the Almighty to perfection?

It is high as heaven, what canft thou do? Deeper than hell, what canft thou know?

The meafure thereof is longer than the earth, and broader than the fea.

If he cut off, and fhut up, or gather together, then who can hinder him?

For he knoweth vain men: he feeth wickednefs alfo; will he not confider it?

If thou prepare thine heart, and stretch out thine hands towards him;

If iniquity be in thine hand, put it far away, and let not wickedness dwell in thy tabernacles.

For then shalt thou lift up thy face without spot; yea, thou shall be stedfast, and not fear.

And thine age shall be clearer than the noon-day; thou shalt shine forth, thou shalt be as the morning.

And thou shalt be secure; thou shalt take thy rest in safety: thou shalt lie down, and none shall make thee afraid.

XII.

SING ye praises unto God; speak of his name; give glory in the highest to the God of our salvation:

Who doeth great things, and unsearchable; marvellous things without number:

Who giveth rain upon the earth, and sendeth waters upon the fields:

Who setteth up on high those that be low; that those who mourn may be exalted to safety.

He disappointeth the devices of the crafty, so that their hands cannot perform their enterprize.

But

But he saveth the poor from the sword, from their mouth, and from the hand of the mighty.

So that the poor hath hope, and iniquity stoppeth her mouth.

Behold, happy is the man whom God correcteth: therefore despise not thou the chastening of the Almighty:

For he maketh sore, and bindeth up; he woundeth, and his hands make whole.

He shall deliver thee in six troubles: yea, in seven there shall no evil touch thee.

In famine he shall redeem thee from death; and in war from the power of the sword.

Thou shalt be hid from the scourge of the tongue; neither shalt thou be afraid of destruction when it cometh.

At destruction and famine thou shalt laugh; neither shalt thou be afraid of the beasts of the earth.

For thou shalt be in league with the stones of the field, and the beasts of the field shall be at peace with thee.

And thou shalt know that thy tabernacle shall be in peace; and thou shalt visit thy habitation, and shalt not sin.

Thou shalt know also that thy seed shall be great, and their offspring, as the grass of the earth.

Thou shalt come to thy grave in a full age, like as a shock of corn cometh in in its season.

Lo this, we have searched it, so it is; hear it, and know thou it for thy good.

XIII.

SURELY there is a vein for the silver, and a place for gold, and by the art of man they are refined.

Iron is taken out of the earth, and copper is molten out of the stone.

The miner contracteth the bounds of darkness, and searcheth out all perfection, even the stones which are concealed in a darkness like the shadow of death.

A torrent suddenly bursteth out from under the inhabitant; even the waters forgotten of the foot: but they are dried up, they are made to vanish away by the skill of man.

Out of the earth cometh bread; and under it is turned up as it were fire.

The stones of it are the place of sapphires; and it hath ore of gold.

This is a path which no eagle knoweth, and which the vulture's eye hath not seen.

The lion's whelps have not trodden it, nor the fierce black lion paffed over it.

The miner putteth forth his hand upon the rock; he overturneth the mountains by the roots.

He cutteth out rivers among the rocks, and his eye feeth every precious thing.

He bindeth the floods from overflowing; and the thing that is hid, bringeth he forth to light.

But where fhall wifdom be found? And where is the place of underftanding?

Man knoweth not the price thereof; neither is it found in the land of the living.

The depth faith, It is not in me: and the fea faith, It is not with me.

It cannot be gotten for gold, neither fhall filver be weighed for the price thereof.

It cannot be valued with the gold of Ophir, with the precious onyx, or the faphire.

The gold and the chryftal cannot equal it: and the exchange fhall not be for jewels of fine gold.

No mention fhall be made of coral, or of pearls: for the price of wifdom is above rubies.

The topaz of Ethiopia fhall not equal it, neither fhall it be valued with pure gold.

Whence then cometh wifdom? And where is the place of underftanding?

Seeing it is hid from the eyes of all living, and kept clofe from the fowls of the air.

Deftruction and Death fay, We have heard the fame thereof with our ears.

God underftandeth the way thereof, and he knoweth the place thereof.

For he looketh to the ends of the earth, and feeth under the whole heaven.

To make the weight for the winds, and he weigheth the waters by meafure.

When he made a decree for the rain, and a way for the lightning of the thunder:

Then did he fee it, and declare it; he prepared it, yea, and fearched it out.

And unto man he faid, Behold, the fear of the Lord, that is wifdom, and to depart from evil is underftanding.

XIV.

BLESSED is the man who maketh the Lord his truft; and refpecteth not the proud, nor fuch as turn afide unto lies.

Bleffed are they that keep judgment, and he that doeth righteoufnefs at all times.

Bleffed

Bleſſed is the man whom thou chaſteneſt, O Lord, and teacheſt him out of thy law.

For the Lord will not caſt off his people; neither will he forſake his inheritance.

When I ſaid, my foot ſlippeth; thy mercy, O Lord, held me up.

In the multitude of my thoughts within me, thy comforts delight my ſoul.

Many, O Lord our God, are thy wonderful works which thou haſt done, and thy thoughts which are to us-ward; they cannot be reckoned up in order unto thee.

If we would declare and ſpeak of them, they are more than can be numbered.

Sacrifice and offering thou didſt not deſire: mine ears haſt thou opened; burnt offering and ſin offering haſt thou not required.

I delight to do thy will, O my God; yea, thy law is within my heart.

Withhold not thy tender mercies from me, O Lord: let thy loving-kindneſs and thy truth continually preſerve me.

Let thy tender mercies come unto me, that I may live; for thy law is my delight.

The Lord is my defence, and my God; the rock of my refuge.

XV.

XV.

BLESSED are the undefiled in the way, who walk in the law of the Lord.

Bleſſed are they that keep his teſtimonies, and that ſeek him with the whole heart.

They alſo do no iniquity: they walk in his ways.

Thou haſt commanded us to keep thy precepts diligently.

O that my ways were directed to keep thy ſtatutes.

Then ſhall I not be aſhamed, when I have reſpect unto all thy commandments.

I will praiſe thee with uprightneſs of heart, when I ſhall have learned thy righteous judgments.

I will keep thy ſtatutes: O forſake me not utterly.

XVI.

WHEREWITH ſhall a young man cleanſe his way?

By taking heed thereto according to thy word.

PART I. MORAL PSALMS.

With my whole heart have I fought thee: O let me not wander from thy commandments.

Thy word have I hid in my heart, that I might not fin againſt thee.

Bleſſed art thou, O Lord: teach me thy ſtatutes.

With my lips have I declared all the judgments of thy mouth.

I have rejoiced in the way of thy teſtimonies, as much as in all riches.

I will meditate in thy precepts, and have reſpect unto thy ways.

I will delight myſelf in thy ſtatutes: I will not forget thy word.

XVII.

EXCEPT the Lord build the houſe, they labour in vain that build it.

Except the Lord keep the city, the watchman waketh but in vain.

It is in vain for you to riſe up early, to ſit up late, to eat the bread of ſorrow; whereas he giveth his beloved ſleep.

Caſt thy burden upon the Lord, and he ſhall ſuſtain thee; he ſhall never ſuffer the righteous to be moved.

Acquaint thyſelf with him, and be at peace.

God

God is the Lord who hath shewed us light.

Thou haft fed us with the fineſt of the wheat; and with honey out of the rock haſt thou ſatisfied us.

It is good for us to draw near unto God: I have put my truſt in the Lord God, that I may declare all thy works.

Truly, God is good unto his people, even to ſuch as be of a clean heart.

Therefore let the righteous be glad: let them rejoice before God; yea, let them exceedingly rejoice.

All they that be fat upon earth, ſhall eat and worſhip: they that go down to the duſt, ſhall bow before him; for none can keep alive his own ſoul.

God is my ſalvation and my glory: the rock of my ſtrength, and my refuge is in God.

The children of thy ſervants ſhall continue, and their ſeed ſhall be eſtabliſhed before thee.

Surely the righteous ſhall give thanks unto thy name; the upright ſhall dwell in thy preſence.

Thus will I bleſs thy name while I live: I will lift up my hands in thy name.

I will remember thee on my bed, and meditate on thee in the night-watches.

My

My tongue also shall talk of thy righteousness all the day long.

We will give thanks unto thee, O Lord, for ever; we will shew forth thy praise to all generations.

PART

PART II.

PSALMS OF PRAISE, PENITENCE, AND PRAYER.

I.

O LORD our Lord, how excellent is thy name in all the earth! who haft fet thy glory above the heavens.

When I confider thy heavens, the work of thy fingers, the moon and the ftars which thou haft ordained:

What is man, that thou art mindful of him? or the fon of man, that thou vifiteft him?

For

For thou haſt made him little lower than the angels, and haſt crowned him with glory and honour.

Thou haſt made him to have dominion over the works of thy hands; thou haſt put all things under his feet:

All ſheep and oxen; yea, and the beaſts of the field:

The fowls of the air, and the fiſh of the ſea, and whatſoever paſſeth through the paths of the ſeas.

O Lord our Lord, how excellent is thy name in all the earth.

II.

I WILL praiſe thee, O Lord, with my whole heart; I will ſhew forth all thy marvellous works.

I will be glad, and rejoice in thee; I will ſing praiſe to thy name, O thou moſt high.

The Lord ſhall endure for ever; he ſhall prepare his throne for judgment.

And he ſhall judge the world in righteouſneſs, he ſhall miniſter judgment to the people in uprightneſs.

The Lord alſo will be a refuge for the oppreſſed, a refuge in time of trouble.

And they that know thy name will put their truſt in thee: for thou, Lord, haſt not forſaken thoſe who ſeek thee.

Sing praiſes to the Lord, who dwelleth in Zion: declare among the people his doings.

The Lord is known by the judgment which he executeth: the wicked is ſnared in the works of his own hands.

The wicked ſhall be turned into hell, and all the nations that forget God.

But the needy ſhall not always be forgotten; the expectation of the poor ſhall not periſh for ever.

III.

PRESERVE me, O God; for in thee do I put my truſt.

O my ſoul, thou haſt ſaid unto the Lord, Thou art my Lord, my goodneſs extendeth not to thee, but to the ſaints that are in the earth, and to the excellent in whom is all my delight.

The Lord is the portion of mine inheritance, and of my cup: thou maintaineſt my lot.

The lines are fallen unto me in pleasant places; yea, I have a goodly heritage.

I have set the Lord always before me: because he is at my right hand, I shall not be moved.

Therefore my heart is glad, and my glory rejoiceth; my flesh also shall rest in hope.

For thou wilt not leave my soul in the grave; neither wilt thou suffer thine holy one to see corruption.

Thou wilt shew me the path of life: in thy presence is fulness of joy, at thy right hand are pleasures for evermore.

IV.

THE heavens declare the glory of God; and the firmament sheweth his handy-work.

Day unto day uttereth speech, and night unto night sheweth knowledge.

They have no speech nor language, yet without these is their voice heard.

Their line is gone out through all the earth, and their words to the end of the world: in them hath he set a tabernacle for the sun.

Which is as a bridegroom coming out of his chamber, and rejoiceth as a strong man to run a race.

His

His going-forth is from the end of the heaven, and his circuit unto the ends of it: and there is nothing hid from the heat thereof.

The law of the Lord is perfect, converting the foul: the teftimony of the Lord is fure, making wife the fimple.

The ftatutes of the Lord are right, rejoicing the heart: the commandment of the Lord is pure, enlightning the eyes.

The fear of the Lord is clean, enduring for ever: the judgments of the Lord are true, and righteous altogether.

More to be defired are they than gold, yea, than much fine gold: fweeter alfo than honey, and the honey-comb.

Moreover, by them is thy fervant warned; and in keeping of them there is great reward.

Who can underftand his errors? Cleanfe thou me from fecret faults.

Keep back thy fervant alfo from prefumptuous fins, let them not have dominion over me: then fhall I be upright, and I fhall be innocent from the great tranfgreffion.

Let the words of my mouth, and the meditation of my heart be acceptable in thy fight, O Lord, my ftrength and my redeemer.

V.

THE Lord is my ſhepherd; I ſhall not want.
He maketh me to lie down in green paſtures: he leadeth me beſide the ſtill waters.

He reſtoreth my ſoul: he leadeth me in the paths of righteouſneſs for his name's ſake.

Yea, though I walk through the valley of the ſhadow of death, I will fear no evil: for thou art with me; thy rod and thy ſtaff they comfort me.

Surely goodneſs and mercy ſhall follow me all the days of my life: and I will dwell in the houſe of the Lord for ever.

VI.

THE earth is the Lord's, and the fulneſs thereof; the world, and they that dwell therein.

For he hath founded it upon the ſeas, and eſtabliſhed it upon the floods.

Who ſhall aſcend into the hill of the Lord? And who ſhall ſtand in his holy place?

He that hath clean hands, and a pure heart; who hath not lift up his ſoul unto vanity, nor ſworn deceitfully, he ſhall receive the bleſſing from the Lord, and righteouſneſs from the God of his ſalvation.

This

This is the generation of them that seek him, that seek thy face, O God of righteousness.

Lift up your heads, O ye gates; and be ye lift up, O ye everlasting doors; and the King of glory shall come in.

Who is the King of glory?

The Lord strong and mighty, the Lord mighty in battle.

Lift up your heads, O ye gates; even lift them up, ye everlasting doors; and the King of glory shall come in.

Who is the King of glory?

The Lord of hosts, he is the King of glory.

VII.

UNTO thee will I cry, O Lord my rock; be not silent unto me; lest if thou be silent unto me, I become like those who go down into the pit.

Hear the voice of my supplications, when I cry unto thee: when I lift up my hands toward thy holy oracle.

Blessed be the Lord, because he hath heard the voice of my supplications.

The Lord is my strength, and my shield; my heart trusted in him, and I am helped: therefore my heart greatly rejoiceth, and with my song will I praise him.

The Lord is my strength; and he is the saving strength of his anointed.

Save thy people, and bless thine inheritance: feed them also, and lift them up for ever.

VIII.

GIVE unto the Lord, ye sons of the mighty, give unto the Lord glory and strength.

Give unto the Lord the glory due unto his name; worship the Lord in the beauty of holiness.

The voice of the Lord is upon the waters: the God of glory thundereth; the Lord is upon many waters.

The voice of the Lord is powerful; the voice of the Lord is full of majesty.

The voice of the Lord breaketh the cedars: yea, the Lord breaketh the cedars of Lebanon.

He maketh them also to skip like a calf: Lebanon and Sirion like a young unicorn.

The voice of the Lord divideth the flames of fire.

The voice of the Lord shaketh the wilderness: the Lord shaketh the wilderness of Kadesh.

The voice of the Lord discovereth the forests; and in his temple doth every one speak of his glory.

The

The Lord fitteth upon the flood; yea, the Lord fitteth King for ever.

The Lord will give strength unto his people; the Lord will bless his people with peace.

IX.

REJOICE in the Lord, O ye righteous; for praise is comely to the upright.

Praise the Lord with harp: sing unto him with the psaltery, and an instrument of ten strings.

Sing unto him a new song, play skilfully with a loud noise.

For the word of the Lord is right: and all his works are done in truth.

He loveth righteousness and judgment: the earth is full of the goodness of the Lord.

By the word of the Lord were the heavens made; and all the host of them by the breath of his mouth.

He gathereth the waters of the sea together, as an heap: he layeth up the depth together in storehouses.

Let all the earth fear the Lord: let all the inhabitants of the world stand in awe of him.

For he spake, and it was done; he commanded, and it stood fast.

The Lord bringeth the counsel of the heathen to nought: he maketh the devices of the people of none effect.

The counsel of the Lord standeth for ever, the thoughts of his heart to all generations.

Blessed is the nation whose God is the Lord; and the people whom he hath chosen for his own inheritance.

The Lord looketh from heaven; he beholdeth all the sons of men.

From the place of his habitation he looketh upon all the inhabitants of the earth.

He fashioneth their hearts alike; he considereth all their works.

There is no king saved by the multitude of an host: a mighty man is not delivered by much strength.

A horse is a vain thing for safety: neither shall he deliver any by his great strength.

Behold, the eye of the Lord is upon them that fear him, upon them that hope in his mercy;

To deliver their soul from death, and to keep them alive in famine.

Our soul waiteth for the Lord: he is our help and our shield.

For our heart shall rejoice in him, because we have trusted in his holy name.

Let

Let thy mercy, O Lord, be upon us, according as we hope in thee.

X.

PRAISE waiteth for thee, O God, in Zion; and unto thee shall the vow be performed.

O thou that hearest prayer, unto thee shall all flesh come.

Blessed is the man whom thou chusest, and causest to approach unto thee, that he may dwell in thy courts.

Blessed be thou, O God, the God of our salvation; who art the confidence of all the ends of the earth, and of them who are afar off upon the sea.

Who by thy strength settest fast the mountains; being girded with power.

Who stilleth the noise of the seas, the noise of their waves, and the tumult of the people.

They also that dwell in the uttermost parts are afraid at thy tokens: thou makest the outgoings of the morning and evening to rejoice.

Thou visitest the earth, and waterest it: thou greatly enrichest it with the river of God, which is full of water: thou preparest corn, when thou hast so provided for it.

Thou watereſt the ridges thereof abundantly: thou ſettleſt the furrows thereof: thou makeſt it ſoft with ſhowers: thou bleſſeſt the ſpringing thereof.

Thou crowneſt the year with thy goodneſs; and thy paths drop fatneſs.

They drop upon the paſtures of the wilderneſs; and the little hills rejoice on every ſide.

The paſtures are clothed with flocks: the vallies alſo are covered over with corn; they ſhout for joy, they alſo ſing.

XI.

MAKE a joyful noiſe unto God, all ye lands. Sing forth the honour of his name: make his praiſe glorious.

Say unto God, How terrible art thou in thy works? Through the greatneſs of thy power ſhall thine enemies ſubmit themſelves unto thee.

All the earth ſhall worſhip thee, and ſhall ſing unto thee; they ſhall ſing to thy name.

Come and ſee the works of God: he is terrible in his doings towards the children of men.

He turned the ſea into dry land: they went through the floods on foot; there did his people rejoice in him.

He

He ruleth by his power for ever; his eyes behold the nations: let not the rebellious exalt themselves.

O blefs our God, ye people; and make the voice of his praife to be heard.

Who holdeth our foul in life, and fuffereth not our feet to be moved.

Come and hear, all ye that fear God, and I will declare what he hath done for my foul.

I cried unto him with my mouth, and he was extolled with my tongue.

If I regard iniquity in my heart, the Lord will not hear me.

But verily God hath heard me; he hath attended to the voice of my prayer.

Bleffed be God, who hath not turned away my prayer, nor his mercy from me.

XII.

GOD be merciful unto us, and blefs us; and caufe thy face to fhine upon us.

That thy name may be known upon the earth, thy faving health among all nations.

Let the people praife thee, O God; let all the people praife thee.

O let the nations be glad, and sing for joy: for thou shall judge the people righteously, and govern the nations upon earth.

Let the people praise thee, O God; let all the people praise thee.

Then shall the earth yield her increase; and God, even our own God, shall bless us.

God shall bless us; and all the ends of the earth shall fear him.

XIII.

THE Lord reigneth, he is clothed with majesty; the Lord is clothed with strength, wherewith he hath girded himself: the world also is stablished, that it cannot be moved.

Thy throne is established of old: thou art from everlasting.

The floods have lifted up, O Lord, the floods have lifted up their voice; the floods lift up their waves.

The Lord on high is mightier than the voice of many waters, yea, than the mighty waves of the sea.

Thy testimonies are very sure: holiness becometh thine house, O Lord, for ever.

XIV.

XIV.

O SING unto the Lord a new song: sing unto the Lord all the earth.

Sing unto the Lord, bless his name; shew forth his salvation from day to day.

Declare his glory among the heathen, his wonders among all people.

For the Lord is great, and greatly to be praised: he is to be feared above all gods.

For all the gods of the nations are idols: but the Lord made the heavens.

Honour and majesty are before him; strength and beauty are in his sanctuary.

Give unto the Lord, O ye kindreds of the people, give unto the Lord glory and strength.

Give unto the Lord the glory due unto his name: bring an offering, and come into his courts.

O worship the Lord in the beauty of holiness: fear before him all the earth.

Say among the heathen, that the Lord reigneth: the world also shall be established that it shall not be moved; he shall judge the people righteously.

Let the heavens rejoice, and the earth be glad: let the sea roar, and the fulness thereof.

Let the field be joyful, and all that is therein: then shall all the trees of the wood rejoice

Before the Lord; for he cometh, for he cometh to judge the earth: he shall judge the world with righteoufnefs, and the people with his truth.

XV.

THE Lord reigneth; let the earth rejoice: let the multitude of ifles be glad thereof.

Clouds and darknefs are round about him: righteoufnefs and judgment are the habitation of his throne.

A fire goeth before him, and burneth up his enemies round about.

His lightnings enlightened the world: the earth faw and trembled.

The hills melted like wax at the prefence of the Lord, at the prefence of the Lord of the whole earth.

The heavens declare his righteoufnefs, and all the people fee his glory.

Confounded be all they that ferve graven images, that boaft themfelves of idols: worfhip him, all ye gods.

Zion heard, and was glad, and the daughters of Judah rejoiced, becaufe of thy judgments, O Lord.

For

For thou, O Lord, art high above all the earth: thou art exalted far above all gods.

Ye that love the Lord, hate evil: he preserveth the souls of his saints; he delivereth them out of the hand of the wicked.

Light is sown for the righteous, and gladness for the upright in heart.

Rejoice in the Lord, ye righteous; and give thanks at the remembrance of his holiness.

XVI.

THE Lord reigneth; let the people tremble: he sitteth between the cherubims; let the earth be moved.

The Lord is great in Zion, and he is above all people.

Let them praise thy great and terrible name; for it is holy.

Exalt ye the Lord our God, and worship at his footstool; for he is holy.

Moses and Aaron among his priests, and Samuel among them that call upon his name: they called upon the Lord, and he answered them.

He spake unto them in the cloudy pillar: they kept his testimonies, and the ordinance that he gave them.

Thou anfweredft them, O Lord our God: thou waft a God that forgaveft them, though thou tookeft vengeance of their inventions.

Exalt the Lord our God, and worfhip at his holy hill: for the Lord our God is holy.

XVII.

MAKE a joyful noife unto the Lord, all ye lands.

Serve the Lord with gladnefs: come before his prefence with finging.

Know ye that the Lord he is God: it is he that hath made us, and not we ourfelves: we are his people, and the fheep of his pafture.

Enter into his gates with thankfgiving, and into his courts with praife: be thankful unto him, and blefs his name.

For the Lord is good: his mercy is everlafting; and his truth endureth to all generations.

XVIII.

O COME let us fing unto the Lord: let us make a joyful noife to the rock of our falvation.

Let

Let us come before his prefence with thankfgiving, and make a joyful noife unto him with pfalms.

For the Lord is a great God, and a great King above all gods.

In his hand are the deep places of the earth: the ftrength of the hills is his alfo.

The fea is his, and he made it: and his hands formed the dry land.

O come, let us worfhip and bow down: let us kneel before the Lord our Maker.

For he is our God; and we are the people of his pafture, and the fheep of his hand.

XIX.

BLESS the Lord, O my foul; and all that is within me, blefs his holy name.

Blefs the Lord, O my foul, and forget not all his benefits.

Who forgiveth all thine iniquities; who healeth all thy difeafes:

Who redeemeth thy life from deftruction; who crowneth thee with loving kindnefs and tender mercies:

Who fatisfieth thy mouth with good things; fo that thy youth is renewed like the eagle's.

The Lord executeth righteousness and judgment for all that are oppressed.

He made known his ways unto Moses, his acts unto the children of Israel.

The Lord is merciful and gracious, slow to anger, and plenteous in mercy.

He will not always chide; neither will he keep his anger for ever.

He hath not dealt with us after our sins; nor rewarded us according to our iniquities.

For as the heaven is high above the earth, so great is his mercy toward them that fear him.

As far as the east is from the west, so far hath he removed our transgressions from us.

Like as a father pitieth his children, so the Lord pitieth them that fear him.

For he knoweth our frame: he remembereth that we are dust.

As for man, his days are as grass: as a flower of the field, so he flourisheth.

For the wind passeth over it, and it is gone; and the place thereof shall know it no more.

But the mercy of the Lord is from everlasting to everlasting upon them that fear him, and his righteousness unto children's children:

To such as keep his covenant, and to those who remember his commandments to do them.

The Lord hath prepared his throne in the heavens; and his kingdom ruleth over all.

Blefs the Lord, ye his angels that excel in ftrength, that do his commandments, hearkening unto the voice of his word.

Blefs the Lord, all ye his hofts; ye minifters of his, that do his pleafure.

Blefs ye the Lord, all his works, in all places of his dominion: blefs the Lord, O my foul.

XX.

BLESS the Lord, O my foul. O Lord my God, thou art very great; thou art clothed with honour and majefty.

Who covereft thyfelf with light, as with a garment: who ftretcheft out the heavens like a curtain.

Who layeth the beams of his chambers in the waters; who maketh the clouds his chariot; who walketh upon the wings of the wind:

Who maketh the winds his meffengers, and flames of fire his minifters:

Who laid the foundations of the earth, that it fhould not be removed for ever.

Thou coveredft it with the deep as with a garment: the waters ftood above the mountains.

At thy rebuke they fled; at the voice of thy thunder they hafted away.

They go up by the mountains; they go down by the vallies, unto the place which thou haſt founded for them.

Thou haſt ſet a bound that they may not paſs over; that they turn not again to cover the earth.

He ſendeth the ſprings into the vallies, which run among the hills.

They give drink to every beaſt of the field: the wild aſſes quench their thirſt.

By them ſhall the fowls of the heaven have their habitation, which ſing among the branches.

He watereth the hills from his chambers: the earth is ſatisfied with the fruit of thy works.

He cauſeth the graſs to grow for the cattle, and herb for the ſervice of man; that he may bring forth food out of the earth:

And wine that maketh glad the heart of man, and oil to make his face to ſhine, and bread to ſtrengthen man's heart.

The trees of the Lord are full of ſap; the cedars of Lebanon which he hath planted;

Where the birds make their neſts: as for the ſtork, the fir-trees are her houſe.

The high hills are a refuge for the wild goats, and the rocks for the conies.

He appointeth the moon for ſeaſons: the ſun knoweth his going down.

Thou makeſt darkneſs, and it is night; wherein all the beaſts of the foreſt do creep forth.

The

The young lions roar after their prey, and seek their meat from God.

The sun ariseth; they gather themselves together, and lay them down in their dens.

Man goeth forth to his work, and to his labour until the evening.

O Lord, how manifold are thy works! in wisdom hast thou made them all: the earth is full of thy riches.

So is the great and wide sea, wherein are things creeping innumerable, both small and great beasts.

There go the ships: there is that leviathan, whom thou hast made to play therein.

These wait all upon thee; that thou mayest give them their meat in due season.

That thou givest them, they gather: thou openest thine hand, they are filled with good.

Thou hidest thy face, they are troubled: thou takest away their breath, they die, and return to their dust.

Thou sendest forth thy spirit, they are created: and thou renewest the face of the earth.

The glory of the Lord shall endure for ever: the Lord shall rejoice in his works.

He looketh on the earth, and it trembleth; he toucheth the hills, and they smoke.

I will sing unto the Lord as long as I live: I will sing praises unto my God while I have my being.

My meditation of him ſhall be ſweet: I will be glad in the Lord.

Let the ſinners be conſumed out of the earth, and let the wicked be no more. Bleſs thou the Lord, O my ſoul. Praiſe ye the Lord.

XXI.

O CLAP your hands, all ye people; ſhout unto God with the voice of triumph.

For the Lord moſt high is terrible: he is a great King over all the earth.

According to thy name, O God, ſo is thy praiſe unto the ends of the earth: thy right hand is full of righteouſneſs.

Sing praiſes to God; ſing praiſes.

For God is the King of all the earth: ſing ye praiſes with underſtanding.

God reigneth over the heathen: God ſitteth upon the throne of his holineſs.

Thy throne, O God, is for ever and ever: the ſceptre of thy kingdom is a right ſceptre.

Great is the Lord, and greatly to be praiſed in the city of our God, in the mountain of his holineſs.

For this God is our God for ever: he will be our guide even unto death.

XXII.

XXII.

BE thou exalted, O God, above the heavens; let thy glory be above all the earth.

My heart is fixed, O God, my heart is fixed: I will sing and give praise.

Thy vows are upon me, O God: I will render praises unto thee.

Awake up my glory, awake psaltery and harp: I myself will awake early.

I will praise thee, O Lord, among the people; I will sing unto thee among the nations.

For thy mercy is great unto the heavens, and thy truth unto the clouds.

Be thou exalted, O God, above the heavens; let thy glory be above all the earth.

XXIII.

PRAISE ye the Lord. Praise God in his sanctuary: praise him in the firmament of his power.

Praise him for his mighty acts: praise him according to his excellent greatness.

Praise him with the sound of the trumpet: praise him with the psaltery and harp.

Praise him with the timbrel and dance: praise him with stringed instruments and organs.

Praise him upon the loud cymbals: praise him upon the high sounding cymbals.

Let every thing that hath breath, praise the Lord. Praise ye the Lord.

XXIV.

SING aloud unto God our strength: make a joyful noise unto the God of Jacob

Take a psalm and bring hither the timbrel, the pleasant harp with the psaltery.

Seek the Lord and his strength, seek his face evermore.

Remember the marvellous works he hath done; his wonders and the judgments of his mouth.

Glory ye in his holy name, let the heart of them rejoice that seek the Lord.

I will remember the works of the Lord: surely I will remember thy wonders of old.

I will meditate also of all thy works, and talk of thy doings.

Thy righteousness also, O God, is very high, who hast done great things: who is like unto thee?

Thou O God hast prepared of thy goodness for the poor.

Thou hast ascended on high, thou hast led captivity captive.

My

My lips shall greatly rejoice when I sing unto thee, and my soul which thou hast redeemed.

I am continually with thee, thou hast holden me by my right hand: God is my helper.

Thou shalt guide me by thy counsel, and afterwards receive me to glory.

XXV.

I WILL praise the name of God with a song, and will magnify him with thankfgiving.

I will also praise thee with the pfaltery, even thy truth, O my God: unto thee will I sing with the harp, O thou holy one of ages.

For thou art my hope O my Lord God, thou art my truft from my youth, by thee have I been holden up from the womb, my praife shall be continually of thee.

Thine hands have made me and fashioned me together round about.

Thou hast clothed me with skin and flesh, and fenced me with bones and sinews.

Thou hast granted me life and favour, and thy visitation hath preserved my spirit.

There is a spirit in man, and the inspiration of the Almighty hath given him understanding.

O God thou hast taught me from my youth, and hitherto have I declared thy wondrous works.

Cast me not off in the time of old age; forsake me not when my strength faileth.

In thee O Lord do I put my trust; let me never be put to confusion.

Let my mouth be filled with thy praise, and with thine honour all the day.

For I will hope continually, and will yet praise thee more and more.

I will go in the strength of the Lord; I will make mention of thy righteousness, even of thine only.

My tongue shall shew forth thy salvation, and thy mercies all the day, for I know not the number thereof.

The Lord is my hope for ever. Amen and Amen.

XXVI.

THE Lord our God is above all lords: strength is his, and glory and power everlasting.

He createth all things by the breath of his mouth: he laid the foundations of the earth, he stretched out the line thereof.

Then the morning stars sang together, and all the sons of God shouted for joy.

God thundereth marvellously with his voice; great things doth he which we cannot comprehend.

He saith to the snow, be thou on the earth;
likewise

likewife to the fmall rain, and to the great rain of his ftrength.

He fealeth up the hand of every man; that all men may know his work.

Then the beafts go into dens, and remain in their places.

Out of the fouth cometh the whirlwind: and cold out of the north.

By the breath of God froft is given: and the breadth of the waters is ftraitened.

Alfo by watering he wearieth the thick cloud: he fcattereth his bright cloud.

And it is turned about by his counfels: that they may do whatfoever he commandeth them upon the face of the earth.

He caufeth it to come, whether for correction, or for his land, or for mercy.

Hearken unto this O man: ftand ftill and confider the wondrous works of God.

But as to the Almighty we cannot find him out: he is beyond all our thoughts.

Behold I go forward, but he is not there; and backward, but I cannot perceive him.

On the left hand where he doth work, but I cannot behold him: he hideth himfelf on the right hand that I cannot fee him.

But he knoweth the way that I take.

For his eyes are upon the ways of man; and he feeth all his goings.

There

There is no darkneſs nor ſhadow of death where the workers of iniquity may hide themſelves.

Shall not his excellency make us afraid? and his dread fall upon us?

Behold, he putteth no truſt in his ſervants; and his angels he chargeth with folly:

How much leſs in them that dwell in houſes of clay, whoſe foundation is in the duſt, who are cruſhed before the moth.

If I be wicked wo unto me; if I be righteous yet will not I lift up mine head.

All my thoughts are before him; according to the multitude of thy mercies, judge thou me, O my God.

XXVII.

O GIVE thanks unto the Lord; for he is good: for his mercy endureth for ever.

O give thanks unto the God of gods: for his mercy endureth for ever.

O give thanks unto the Lord of lords: for his mercy endureth for ever.

To him who alone doeth great wonders: for his mercy endureth for ever.

To him that by wiſdom made the heavens: for his mercy endureth for ever.

To him that ſtretched out the earth above the waters:

waters: for his mercy endureth for ever.

To him that made great lights: for his mercy endureth for ever.

The sun to rule by day: for his mercy endureth for ever.

The moon and stars to rule by night: for his mercy endureth for ever.

Even an heritage unto Israel his servant: for his mercy endureth for ever.

Who remembered us in our low estate: for his mercy endureth for ever.

And hath redeemed us from our enemies: for his mercy endureth for ever.

Who giveth food to all flesh: for his mercy endureth for ever.

O give thanks unto the God of heaven: for his mercy endureth for ever.

XXVIII.

PRAISE ye the Lord. Sing unto the Lord a new song, and his praise in the congregations of saints.

Let man rejoice in him that made him: let the children of men be joyful in their King.

Let them praise his name in the dance: let them sing praises unto him with the timbrel and harp.

For the Lord taketh pleasure in his people: he will

will beautify the meek with salvation. Praise ye the Lord.

XXIX.

PRAISE the Lord: for it is good to sing praises unto our God; for it is pleasant, and praise is comely.

Great is our Lord, and of great power: his understanding is infinite.

The Lord lifteth up the meek: he casteth the wicked down to the ground.

He healeth the broken in heart, and bindeth up their wounds.

He telleth the number of the stars; he calleth them all by their names.

Sing unto the Lord with thanksgiving: sing praises upon the harp to our God.

Who covereth the heaven with clouds, who prepareth rain for the earth, who maketh grass to grow upon the mountains.

He giveth to the beast his food, and to the young ravens which cry.

He delighteth not in the strength of the horse: he taketh not pleasure in the vigour of a man.

The Lord taketh pleasure in them that fear him, in those that hope in his mercy.

Part II. PENITENCE, AND PRAYER.

Praife the Lord, O ye nations: praife thy God, O Britain.

For he hath ftrengthened the bars of thy gates; he hath bleffed thy children within thee.

He maketh peace in thy borders, and filleth thee with the fineft of the wheat.

He fendeth forth his commandment upon earth: his word runneth very fwiftly.

He giveth fnow like wool: he fcattereth the hoar froft like afhes.

He cafteth forth his ice like morfels: who can ftand before his cold?

He fendeth out his word, and melteth them: he caufeth his wind to blow, and the waters flow.

He fheweth his word unto Britain, his ftatutes and his judgments unto his people.

He hath not dealt fo with every nation: and as for his judgments, they have not known them. Praife ye the Lord.

XXX.

PRAISE ye the Lord. Praife ye the Lord from the heavens: praife him in the heights.

Praife ye him, all his angels: praife ye him, all his hofts.

Praife ye him, fun and moon: praife him, all ye ftars of light.

Praife him, ye heavens of heavens, and ye waters that be above the heavens.

Let them praife the name of the Lord: for he commanded, and they were created.

He alfo eftablifhed them for ever and ever: he hath made a decree which fhall not pafs.

Praife the Lord from the earth, ye dragons, and all deeps.

Fire and hail, fnow and vapour, ftormy wind fulfilling his word:

Mountains, and all hills; fruitful trees, and all cedars:

Beafts, and all cattle; creeping things, and flying fowl:

Kings of the earth, and all people; princes, and all judges of the earth:

Both young men, and maidens; old men, and children.

Let them praife the name of the Lord: for his name alone is excellent; his glory is above the earth and heaven.

XXXI.

PRAISE ye the Lord. Praife the Lord, O my foul.

While I live will I praife the Lord: I will fing praifes unto my God while I have any being.

Put

Put not your trust in princes, nor in the son of man, in whom there is no help.

His breath goeth forth, he returneth to his earth: in that very day his thoughts perish.

Happy is he that hath the God of Jacob for his help, whose hope is in the Lord his God:

Who made heaven and earth, the sea, and all that therein is:

Who keepeth truth for ever: Who executeth judgment for the oppressed, who giveth food to the hungry.

The Lord looseth the prisoners: The Lord openeth the eyes of the blind:

The Lord raiseth them that are bowed down: the Lord loveth the righteous:

The Lord preserveth the strangers; he relieveth the fatherless and widow: but he overturneth the way of the wicked.

The Lord shall reign for ever; even thy God, O Zion, unto all generations. Praise ye the Lord.

XXXII.

I WILL extol thee, my God, O King; and I will bless thy name for ever and ever.

Every day will I bless thee; and I will praise thy name for ever and ever.

Great is the Lord, and greatly to be praised; and his greatness is unsearchable.

One generation shall praise thy works to another, and shall declare thy mighty acts.

I will speak of the glorious honours of thy majesty, and of thy wondrous works.

And men shall speak of the might of thy terrible acts: and I will declare thy greatness.

They shall abundantly utter the memory of thy great goodness, and shall sing of thy righteousness.

The Lord is gracious, and full of compassion; slow to anger, and of great mercy.

The Lord is good to all: and his tender mercies are over all his works.

All thy works shall praise thee, O Lord, and thy saints shall bless thee.

They shall speak of the glory of thy kingdom, and talk of thy power.

To make known to the sons of men thy mighty acts, and the glorious majesty of thy kingdom.

Thy kingdom is an everlasting kingdom, and thy dominion endureth throughout all generations.

The Lord upholdeth all that fall, and raiseth up all those that be bowed down.

The eyes of all wait upon thee, and thou givest them their meat in due season.

Thou openest thine hand, and satisfiest the desire of every living thing.

The Lord is righteous in all his ways, and holy in all his works.

The Lord is nigh unto all who call upon him, to all who call upon him in truth.

He will fulfil the defire of them that fear him: he alfo will hear their cry, and will fave them.

The Lord preferveth all them that love him: but all the wicked will he deftroy.

My mouth fhall fpeak the praife of the Lord: and let all flefh blefs his holy name for ever and ever.

XXXIII.

PRAISE ye the Lord. O ye fervants of the Lord, praife the name of the Lord.

O praife the Lord all ye nations: praife him all ye people.

Bleffed be the name of the Lord, from this time forth and for evermore.

For his merciful kindnefs is great towards us; and the truth of the Lord endureth for ever.

From the rifing of the fun until the going down of the fame, the Lord's name is to be praifed.

The Lord is high above all nations, and his glory above all the heavens.

Who is like unto the Lord our God, who dwelleth on high.

Who humbleth himfelf to behold the things that are in heaven, and in the earth?

He raiseth up the poor out of the dust, and lifteth the needy out of the dunghill.

That he may set him with princes, even the princes of his people.

He maketh the barren woman to keep house, and to be a joyful mother of children. Praise ye the Lord.

XXXIV.

PRAISE ye the Lord. I will praise the Lord with my whole heart, in the assembly of the upright, and in the congregation.

The works of the Lord are great, sought out of all them that have pleasure therein.

His work is honourable and glorious: and his righteousness endureth for ever.

He hath made his wonderful works to be remembered; the Lord is gracious and full of compassion.

He hath given meat unto them that fear him: he will ever be mindful of his covenant.

He hath shewed his people the power of his works, that he may give them a heritage in a good land.

The works of his hands are verity and judgment: all his commandments are sure.

They stand fast for ever and ever, and are done in truth and uprightness.

He sent redemption unto his people, he hath commanded

commanded his covenant for ever: holy and reverend is his name.

The fear of the Lord is the beginning of wifdom: a good underftanding have all they that do his commandments: his praife endureth for ever.

XXXV.

O GIVE thanks unto the Lord, for he is good: for his mercy endureth for ever.

Let the redeemed of the Lord fay fo, whom he hath redeemed from the hand of the enemy;

And gathered them out of the lands, from the eaft and from the weft, from the north and from the fouth.

They wandered in the wildernefs in a folitary way, they found no city to dwell in.

Hungry and thirfty, their foul fainted in them.

Then they cried unto the Lord in their trouble, and he delivered them out of their diftreffes.

And he led them forth by the right way, that they might go to a city of habitation.

Oh that men would praife the Lord for his goodnefs, and for his wonderful works, to the children of men!

For he fatisfieth the longing foul, and filleth the hungry foul with goodnefs.

Such as sit in darkness, and in the shadow of death, being bound in affliction and iron:

Because they rebelled against the words of God, and contemned the counsel of the most High:

Therefore he brought down their heart with labour, they fell down, and there was none to help.

Then they cried unto the Lord in their trouble, and he saved them out of their distresses.

He brought them out of darkness, and the shadow of death, and brake their bands in sunder.

Oh that men would praise the Lord for his goodness, and for his wonderful works to the children of men!

For he hath broken the gates of brass, and cut the bars of iron in sunder.

Fools, because of their transgression, and because of their iniquities, are afflicted.

Their soul abhorreth all manner of meat, and they draw near unto the gates of death.

Then they cry unto the Lord in their trouble, he saveth them out of their distresses.

He sent his word, and healed them, and delivered them from their destructions.

Oh that men would praise the Lord for his goodness, and for his wonderful works to the children of men!

And let them sacrifice the sacrifices of thanksgiving, and declare his work with rejoicing.

They

They that go down to the sea in ships, that do business in great waters:

These see the works of the Lord, and his wonders in the deep.

For he commandeth, and raiseth the stormy wind, which lifteth up the waves thereof.

They mount up to the heaven, they go down again to the depths, their soul is melted because of trouble.

Thy reel to and fro, and stagger like a drunken man, and are at their wit's end.

Then they cry unto the Lord in their trouble, and he bringeth them out of their distresses.

He maketh the storm a calm, so that the waves thereof are still.

Then are they glad, because they be quiet; so he bringeth them unto their desired haven.

Oh that men would praise the Lord for his goodness, and for his wonderful works to the children of men!

Let them exalt him also in the congregation of the people, and praise him in the assembly of the elders.

He turneth rivers into a wilderness, and the water-springs into dry ground:

A fruitful land into barrenness for the wickedness of them that dwell therein.

He turneth the wildernefs into a ftanding water, and dry ground into water-fprings.

And there he maketh the hungry to dwell, that that may prepare a city for habitation;

And fow the fields, and plant vineyards, which may yield fruits of increafe.

Again they are diminifhed and brought low through oppreffion, affliction, and forrow.

He poureth contempt upon princes, and caufeth them to wander in the wildernefs, where there is no way.

Yet fetteth he the poor on high from affliction, and maketh him families like a flock.

The righteous fhall fee it, and rejoice; and all iniquity fhall ftop her mouth.

Whofo is wife, and will obferve thefe things, even they fhall underftand the loving kindnefs of the Lord.

XXXVI.

I WILL blefs the Lord at all times: his praife fhall continually be in my mouth.

My foul fhall make her boaft in the Lord: the humble fhall hear thereof and be glad.

O magnify the Lord with me, and let us exalt his name together.

O tafte

Part II. PENITENCE, AND PRAYER.

O taste and see that the Lord is good: blessed is the man that trusteth in him.

O fear the Lord, ye his saints: for there is no want to them that fear him.

The young lions do lack, and suffer hunger: but they that seek the Lord shall not want any good thing.

Come ye children hearken unto me: I will teach you the fear of the Lord.

What man is he that desireth life, and loveth many days, that he may see good?

Keep thy tongue from evil, and do good: seek peace and pursue it.

The eyes of the Lord are upon the righteous, and his ears are open unto their cry.

The face of the Lord is against them that do evil, to cut off the remembrance of them from the earth.

The righteous cry, and the Lord heareth, and delivereth them out of all their troubles.

The Lord is nigh unto them that are of a broken heart, and saveth such as be of a contrite spirit.

Many are the afflictions of the righteous: but the Lord delivereth him out of them all.

He keepeth all his bones: not one of them is broken.

Evil shall slay the wicked: and they that hate the righteous shall be desolate.

He

He redeemeth the foul of his fervants: and none of them that truft in him fhall be defolate.

XXXVII.

BLESS ye God in the congregations.

Sing unto God, fing praifes to his name: extol him that rideth upon the heavens by his name JEHOVAH, and rejoice before him.

O God when thou wenteft forth before thy people, the earth fhook, the heavens alfo dropped at the prefence of God.

At the prefence of God the earth trembled: the foundations alfo of the hills moved, and were fhaken.

He bowed the heavens and came down: and darknefs was under his feet.

And he rode upon a cherub, and did fly: yea, he did fly upon the wings of the wind.

He made darknefs his fecret place; his pavillion round about him was dark waters and thick clouds of the fkies.

Thy mercy, O God, is in the heavens; and thy faithfulnefs reacheth unto the clouds.

Thy righteoufnefs is like the great mountains; thy judgments are a great deep: O Lord, thou preferveft man and beaft.

How excellent is thy loving kindnefs, O God! therefore the children of men put their truft under the fhadow of thy wings.

They

They shall be abundantly satisfied with the fatness of thy house; and thou shalt make them drink of the rivers of thy pleasures.

For with thee is the fountain of life: in thee shall we see light.

O continue thy loving kindness to them that know thee; and thy righteousness to the upright in heart.

Blessed be the Lord, who daily loadeth us with benefits; even the God of our salvation.

Blessed be the Lord God of Israel, from everlasting to everlasting. Amen and Amen.

XXXVIII.

IT is a good thing to give thanks unto the Lord, and to sing praises unto thy name, O thou most high:

To shew forth thy loving-kindness in the morning, and thy faithfulness every night;

Upon an instrument of ten strings, and upon the psaltery; upon the harp with a solemn sound.

For thou, Lord, hast made me glad through thy work: I will triumph in the works of thy hands.

O Lord, how great are thy works! And thy thoughts are very deep.

A brutish man knoweth not; neither doth a fool understand this.

When

When the wicked spring as the grafs, and when all the workers of iniquity do flourish; it is that they shall be destroyed for ever.

But thou, Lord, art most high for evermore.

For lo, thine enemies, O Lord, for lo, thine enemies shall perish; all the workers of iniquity shall be scattered.

The righteous shall flourish like the palm-tree: he shall grow like a cedar in Lebanon.

These that be planted in the house of the Lord, shall flourish in the courts of our God.

They shall bring forth fruit in old age; they shall be fat and flourishing:

To shew that the Lord is upright: he is their rock, and there is no unrighteousness in him.

XXXIX.

PRAISE ye the Lord, praise ye the name of the Lord; praise him, O ye servants of the Lord.

Ye that stand in the house of the Lord, in the courts of the house of our God.

Praise ye the Lord, for the Lord is good: sing praise unto his name, for it is pleasant.

For the Lord hath chosen his people unto himself, and his redeemed for a peculiar treasure.

For I know that the Lord is great, and that our Lord is above all gods.

Whatsoever the Lord pleaseth, that doth he in heaven, and in earth, in the seas, and all deep places.

He causeth the vapours to ascend from the ends of the earth: he maketh lightnings for the rain: he bringeth the wind out of his treasures.

Thy name, O Lord, endureth for ever, and thy memorial to all generations.

The idols of the heathens are silver and gold, the work of men's hands.

They have mouths, but they speak not; eyes have they, but they see not; ears have they, but they hear not; neither is there any breath in their mouths.

They that make them are like unto them: so is every one that trusteth in them.

But thy name, O Lord, endureth for ever; and thy memorial unto all generations.

XL.

CAN man be just with God? Can a man be pure before his Maker?

If he will contend with him, he cannot answer him for one of a thousand.

He is wise in heart, and mighty in strength: who hath hardened himself against him, and hath prospered?

Who removeth the mountains, and they know not: who overturneth them in his anger.

Who shaketh the earth out of her place, and the pillars thereof tremble.

Who commandeth the sun, and it riseth not; and sealeth up the stars.

Who alone spreadeth out the heavens, and treadeth upon the waves of the sea.

Who maketh Arcturus, Orion, and Pleiades, and the chambers of the south.

Who doeth great things past finding out; yea, and wonders without number.

Lo, he goeth by me, and I see him not: he passeth on also, but I perceive him not.

Behold, he taketh away, who can hinder him? Who will say unto him, What doest thou?

If we speak of strength, lo, he is strong: and if of judgment, who is a King beside our God?

Whoso justifieth himself, his own mouth shall condemn him. If thou say thou art perfect, it shall also prove thee perverse.

How then can man be justified with God? Or how can he be clean that is born of a woman?

Behold, he looketh even to the moon, and it shineth not; yea, the stars are not pure in his sight.

How much less man, who is of the dust; and the son of man, who is a worm?

XLI.

XLI.

THE Lord our God is an everlasting King; mighty is his arm, and strong is his right arm.

Praise ye the Lord our God: he is great, and doeth wondrous things; he is God alone.

Hell is naked before him, and destruction hath no covering.

He stretcheth out the north over the empty place, and hangeth the earth upon nothing.

He bindeth up the waters in his thick clouds; and the cloud is not rent under them.

He holdeth back the face of his throne, and spreadeth his cloud upon it.

He hath compassed the waters with bounds, until the day and night come to an end.

The pillars of heaven tremble, and are astonished at his reproof.

He divideth the sea with his power, and by his understanding he smiteth through the proud.

By his spirit he hath garnished the heavens: his hand hath formed the crooked serpent.

Lo, these are parts of his ways: yet how little a portion is heard of him? But the thunder of his power who can understand?

XLII.

XLII.

PRAISE ye the Lord. O give thanks unto the Lord; for he is good: for his mercy endureth for ever.

O give thanks unto the Lord; call upon his name: make known his deeds among the people.

Sing unto him, sing psalms unto him: talk ye of all his wondrous works.

He hath remembered his covenant for ever, the word which he spake to a thousand generations.

Ye that fear the Lord, praise him: all ye the seed of Zion glorify him; and fear him all ye seed of his chosen ones.

For he hath not despised nor abhorred the affliction of the afflicted: neither hath he hid his face from him; but when he cried unto him he heard.

The Lord will maintain the cause of the afflicted, and the right of the poor.

The meek shall eat, and be satisfied: they shall praise the Lord that seek him; their heart shall live for ever.

All the ends of the world shall remember and turn unto the Lord: and all the kindreds of the nations shall worship before him.

For the Lord heareth the poor, and despiseth not his prisoners.

Verily there is a reward for the righteous: verily there is a God who judgeth in the earth.

The humble shall hear this, and be glad: and their heart shall live that seek God.

XLIII.

I WILL lift up mine eyes unto the hills, from whence cometh my help.

My help cometh from the Lord, who made heaven and earth.

He will not suffer thy foot to be moved: he that keepeth thee will not slumber.

Behold, he that keepeth Israel, shall neither slumber nor sleep.

The Lord is thy keeper: the Lord is thy shade upon thy right hand.

The sun shall not smite thee by day, nor the moon by night.

The Lord shall preserve thee from all evil: he shall preserve thy soul.

The Lord shall preserve thy going out, and thy coming in, from this time forth, and even for evermore.

XLIV.

GIVE ear, O shepherd of Israel, thou that leadest thy people like a flock; thou that dwelledst between the cherubims, shine forth.

O God my heart is fixed, I will sing and give praise.

Awake psaltery and harp: I myself will awake early.

I will praise thee O Lord among the people: I will sing praises unto thee among the nations.

For thy mercy is great above the heavens; and thy truth reacheth unto the clouds.

Thou O Lord art a shield for me; my glory and the lifter up of mine head.

Salvation belongeth unto the Lord: thy blessing is upon thy people.

Be thou exalted, O God, above the heavens, and thy glory above all the earth.

Blessed be the Lord God of Israel from everlasting to everlasting: and let all the people say, Amen.

Amen, praise ye the Lord.

XLV.

I WILL sing of mercy and judgment: unto thee, O Lord, will I sing.

God is my king of old; working salvation in the midst of the earth.

Thou didst divide the sea by thy strength: thou didst cleave the fountain and the flood: thou driedst up mighty rivers.

The day is thine, the night also is thine: thou hast prepared the light and the sun.

Thou hast set all the borders of the earth: thou hast made summer and winter.

According to thy name, O God, so is thy praise, to the ends of the earth: thy right hand is full of righteousness.

O let not the oppressed return ashamed: let the poor and needy praise thy name.

Defend the poor and fatherless: do justice to the afflicted and needy.

Deliver the poor and needy: rid them out of the hand of the wicked.

Let the sighing of the prisoner come before thee: and the prayer of the desolate that hath none to help.

Arise, O God, judge the earth: for thou shalt inherit all nations.

That men may know that thou, whose name alone

is Jehovah, art the moſt High over all the earth.
Ariſe O God, plead thine own cauſe.

XLVI.

I WILL ſing of the mercies of the Lord for ever: with my mouth will I make known thy faithfulneſs unto all generations.

For I have ſaid, mercy ſhall be built up for ever: thy faithfulneſs ſhall thou eſtabliſh in the very heavens.

And the heavens ſhall praiſe thy wonders, O Lord: thy faithfulneſs alſo in the congregations of the ſaints.

For who in the heaven can be compared unto the Lord? who among the ſons of the mighty can be likened unto the Lord our God?

God is greatly to be feared in the aſſembly of his ſaints, and to be had in reverence of all them that are about him.

O Lord God of hoſts, who is a ſtrong Lord like unto thee? or what is like unto thy faithfulneſs round about thee?

Thou ruleſt the raging of the ſea: when the waves thereof ariſe, thou ſtilleſt them.

The heavens are thine, the earth alſo is thine: as for the world, and the fulneſs thereof, thou haſt founded them.

Thou

Thou haſt a mighty arm: ſtrong is thy hand, and high is thy right hand.

Juſtice and judgment are the habitation of thy throne: mercy and truth ſhall go before thy face.

Bleſſed is the people that know the joyful ſound: they ſhall walk, O Lord, in the light of thy countenance.

In thy name ſhall they rejoice all the day; and in thy righteouſneſs ſhall they be exalted.

For the Lord is our defence; and the Holy One of Iſrael is our King.

Bleſſed be the Lord for evermore. Amen and Amen.

XLVII.

I WILL love thee, O Lord my ſtrength.

The Lord is my rock, and my fortreſs, and my deliverer; my God, my ſtrength, in whom I will truſt; my buckler, and the horn of my ſalvation, and my high tower.

I will ſing unto the Lord, becauſe he hath dealt bountifully with me.

I will call upon the Lord, who is worthy to be praiſed: our fathers truſted in thee, they truſted and thou didſt deliver them.

For who is God ſave the Lord? or who is a rock ſave our God.

It is God that girdeth me with strength, and maketh my way perfect.

Thou haſt alſo given me the ſhield of thy ſalvation: and thy right hand hath holden me up, and thy gentleneſs hath made me great.

For thou wilt ſave the afflicted people; but wilt bring down high looks.

With the merciful thou will ſhew thyſelf merciful; with an upright man thou wilt ſhew thyſelf upright.

With the pure thou wilt ſhew thyſelf pure; and with the froward thou wilt ſhew thyſelf froward.

Thy way O God is perfect: the word of the Lord is tried, he is a buckler to all thoſe that truſt in him.

I will give thanks unto thee, O Lord, among the people, and ſing praiſes unto thy name.

The Lord liveth, and bleſſed be my rock; and let the God of my ſalvation be exalted.

XLVIII.

INTO thine hand I commit my ſpirit: thou haſt redeemed me, O Lord God of truth.

O how great is thy goodneſs, which thou haſt laid up for thoſe who fear thee, which thou haſt wrought for thoſe who truſt in thee before the ſons of men.

Thou

Thou shalt hide them in the secret of thy presence from the pride of man: thou shalt keep them secretly in a pavilion from the strife of tongues.

Many sorrows shall be to the wicked; but he that trusteth in the Lord, mercy shall compass him about.

O love the Lord, ye his saints; for the Lord preserveth the faithful, and plentifully rewardeth the proud doer.

Be glad in the Lord, and rejoice, ye righteous; and shout, all ye that are upright in heart.

We have thought of thy loving kindness, O God, in the midst of thy temple.

In God we boast all the day long, and praise thy name for ever.

My soul, wait thou only upon God; for my expectation is from him.

Whom have I in heaven but thee? And there is none upon earth that I desire besides thee.

My flesh and my heart shall fail; but God is the strength of my heart, and my portion for ever.

XLIX.

SING unto God, O ye kingdoms of the earth: O sing praises unto the Lord.

To him who rideth upon the heavens of heavens,

which were of old: lo, he doth send out his voice, and that a mighty voice.

Ascribe ye strength unto God. O God, thou art terrible out of thy holy places: the Lord of hosts is he who giveth strength and power unto his people. Blessed be his name.

The wicked say, How doth God know? Is there knowledge in the Most High?

He that planted the ear, shall he not hear? He that formed the eye, shall he not see?

He that chastiseth the heathen, shall he not correct? He that teacheth man knowledge, shall he not know?

The Lord knoweth the thoughts of man, that they are vanity.

But thou art holy, O thou that inhabitest the praises of Israel.

Who can utter the mighty acts of the Lord? who can shew forth all thy praise?

Let the heaven and earth praise thee; the seas, and every thing that moveth therein.

Let all those who seek thee rejoice, and be glad in thee: and let such as love thy salvation say continually, The Lord be magnified. Amen and Amen.

L.

L.

UNTO thee, O God, do we give thanks: unto thee do we give thanks; for that thy name is near, thy wondrous works do shew forth.

Thou, even thou art to be feared; and who may stand in thy sight, when once thou art angry.

Thou didst cause judgment to be heard from heaven; the earth feared, and was still.

Thy way, O God, is in the sanctuary: who is so great a god as our God.

Thou art the God that doest wonders; thou hast declared thy strength among the people.

Thou with thine arm didst redeem thy people of old.

The waters saw thee, O God, the waters saw thee; they were afraid: the depths also were troubled.

The clouds poured out water, the skies sent out a sound, thine arrows also went abroad.

The voice of thy thunder was in the heavens, thy lightnings enlightened the world, the earth trembled and shook.

Thy way is in the sea, and thy path in the great waters, and thy footsteps are not known.

Of old hast thou laid the foundations of the earth, and the heavens are the works of thy hands.

They shall perish, but thou shalt endure.

Yea,

Yea, all of them ſhall wax old as a garment; as a veſture ſhalt thou change them, and they ſhall be changed.

But thou art the ſame, and thy years ſhall have no end.

Our days are like a ſhadow which declineth, and we are withered like graſs.

The earth, and all the inhabitants thereof, ſhall be diſſolved.

But thou, O God, ſhalt endure for ever, and thy memorial unto all generations.

The children of thy ſervants ſhall continue, and their ſeed ſhall be eſtabliſhed before thee.

For the kingdom is the Lord's; he is the governor among the nations.

He is the Lord our God; his judgments are in all the earth.

LI.

MAKE a joyful noiſe unto the Lord, all the earth: make a loud noiſe, and rejoice and ſing praiſe.

Sing unto the Lord with the harp; with the harp, and the voice of a pſalm.

With trumpets and ſound of cornet make a joyful noiſe before the Lord the King.

Let

Let the sea roar, and the fulness thereof; the world, and they that dwell therein.

Let the floods clap their hands: let the hills be joyful together

Before the Lord: for he cometh to judge the earth: with righteousness shall he judge the world, and the people with equity.

LII.

O GIVE thanks unto the Lord; for he is good: for his mercy endureth for ever.

Let those who fear the Lord say, that his mercy endureth for ever.

Their God is on their side, they will not fear what man can do unto them.

They shall not die, but live, and declare the works of him that helped them.

It is better to trust in the Lord, than to put confidence in man.

It is better to trust in the Lord, than to put confidence in princes.

The Lord is my strength and my song, and he is become my salvation.

The voice of rejoicing and salvation is in the tabernacles of the righteous. The right hand of the Lord is exalted.

Salvation

Salvation is far from the wicked; for they seek not thy statutes.

Great are thy tender mercies, O Lord: quicken me according to thy judgment.

Thy word is very pure, therefore thy servant loveth it.

Thy righteousness is an everlasting righteousness, and thy word is the truth.

Thy word is true from the beginning, and every one of thy righteous judgments endureth for ever.

Great peace have they who love thy law, and nothing shall offend them.

Thou art my God, and I will praise thee; my father's God, I will exalt thee.

O give thanks unto the Lord; for he is good: for his mercy endureth for ever.

LIII.

O LORD, thou hast searched me and known me.

Thou knowest my down-sitting, and my uprising; thou understandest my thoughts afar off.

Thou compassest my path, and my lying down, and art acquainted with all my ways.

For there is not a word in my tongue, but lo, O Lord, thou knowest it altogether.

Thou

Part II. PENITENCE, AND PRAYER.

Thou haſt beſet me behind and before, and laid thine hand upon me.

Such knowledge is too wonderful for me, it is high, I cannot attain unto it.

Whither ſhall I go from thy ſpirit? or whither ſhall I flee from thy preſence?

If I aſcend up into heaven, thou art there: if I make my bed in hell, behold thou art there.

If I take the wings of the morning, and dwell in the uttermoſt parts of the ſea;

Even there ſhall thy hand lead me, and thy right hand ſhall hold me.

If I ſay, ſurely the darkneſs ſhall cover me; even the night ſhall be light about me.

Yea, the darkneſs hideth not from thee; but the night ſhineth as the day: the darkneſs and the light are both alike to thee.

For thou haſt poſſeſſed my reins: thou haſt covered me in my mother's womb.

I will praiſe thee, for I am fearfully and wonderfully made; marvellous are thy works, and that my ſoul knoweth right well.

My ſubſtance was not hid from thee, when I was made in ſecret, and curiouſly wrought in the loweſt parts of the earth.

Thine eyes did ſee my ſubſtance yet being imperfect, and in thy book all my members were written,

written, which in continuance were fashioned, when as yet there was none of them.

How precious also are thy thoughts unto me, O God! how great is the sum of them!

If I should count them, they are more in number than the sand: when I awake, I am still with thee.

Search me, O God, and know my heart: try me, and know my thoughts.

And see if there be any wicked way in me, and lead me in the way everlasting.

LIV.

THE Lord is my light and my salvation, whom shall I fear?

The Lord is the strength of my life, of whom shall I be afraid?

Though an host should encamp against me, my heart shall not fear: though war should rise against me, in this will I be confident.

For in the time of trouble he shall hide me in his pavilion: in the secret of his tabernacle shall he hide me; he shall set me upon a rock.

Therefore will I offer in his tabernacle sacrifices of joy; I will sing, yea, I will sing praises unto the Lord.

Hear, O Lord, when I cry with my voice: have mercy also upon me, and answer me.

Part II. PENITENCE, AND PRAYER.

When thou saidst, Seek ye my face; my heart said unto thee, Thy face, Lord, will I seek.

Hide not thy face far from me; put not thy servant away in anger: thou hast been my help, leave me not, neither forsake me, O God of my salvation.

When my father and my mother forsake me, then the Lord will take me up.

I had fainted, unless I had believed to see the goodness of the Lord in the land of the living.

Wait on the Lord, be of good courage, and he shall strengthen thine heart: wait, I say, on the Lord.

LV.

O LORD, attend unto my cry; give ear unto my prayer, that goeth not out of feigned lips.

Hold up my goings in thy paths, that my footsteps slip not.

I have called upon thee, for thou wilt hear me, O God: incline thine heart unto me, and hear my speech.

Shew thy marvellous loving-kindness, O thou that savest by thy right hand those who put their trust in thee.

That I may publish with the voice of thanksgiving, and tell of all thy wondrous works.

Keep

Keep me as the apple of the eye, take me under the shadow of thy wings.

O satisfy us early with thy mercy, that we may rejoice, and be glad all our days.

Let thy work appear unto thy servant, and thy glory unto their children.

And let the beauty of the Lord our God be upon us: and establish thou the work of our hands upon us; yea, the work of our hands establish thou it.

LVI.

HEAR me when I call, O God of my righteousness: have mercy upon me and hear my prayer.

The Lord hath set apart him that is godly for himself: the Lord will hear when he calleth upon him.

Stand in awe, and sin not: commune with your own heart and be still.

Offer the sacrifices of righteousness; and put your trust in the Lord.

There be many that say, who will shew us any good?

Lord lift thou up the light of thy countenance upon us.

Thou hast put gladness in my heart, more than

in

in the time when their corn and their wine increased.

I will both lay me down in peace, and sleep: for thou, Lord, only makest me dwell in safety.

LVII.

BOW down thine ear, O Lord, hear me; for I am poor and needy.

Preserve my soul: O thou my God, save thy servant that trusteth in thee.

Be merciful unto me, O Lord; for I cry unto thee daily.

Rejoice the soul of thy servant; for unto thee, O Lord, do I lift up my soul.

For thou, O Lord, art good, and ready to forgive; and plenteous in mercy unto all them that call upon thee.

Give ear, O Lord, unto my prayer; and attend to the voice of my supplications.

In the day of my trouble I will call upon thee, for thou wilt answer me.

Among the gods there is none like unto thee, O Lord; neither are there any works like unto thy works.

All nations whom thou hast made, shall come and worship before thee, O Lord, and shall glorify thy name.

For thou art great, and doſt wondrous things: thou art God alone.

Teach me thy way, O Lord; I will walk in thy truth: incline my heart to fear thy name.

I will praiſe thee, O Lord my God, with all my heart: and I will glorify thy name for evermore.

For great is thy mercy toward me; and thou haſt delivered my ſoul from the loweſt hell.

But thou, O Lord, art a God full of compaſſion, and gracious; long-ſuffering, and plenteous in mercy and truth.

O turn unto me, and have mercy upon me: give thy ſtrength unto thy ſervant, and ſave the ſon of thine handmaid.

So will I praiſe thy name alway; thy praiſe ſhall continually be upon my lips.

LVIII.

UNTO thee do we lift up our eyes, O thou that dwelleſt in the heavens.

Hear our prayer, O Lord, give ear to our ſupplications: in thy faithfulneſs anſwer us, and in thy righteouſneſs.

Behold, as the eyes of ſervants look unto the hand of their maſter, and as the eyes of a maiden unto the hand of her miſtreſs; ſo our eyes wait upon

Part II. PENITENCE, AND PRAYER.

on the Lord our God, till that he have mercy upon us.

O enter not into judgment with thy servants, for in thy sight shall no man living be justified.

I remember the days of old, I meditate on all thy works: I muse on the works of thy hands.

I stretch forth my hands unto thee: my soul thirsteth after thee, as a thirsty land.

Hear us speedily, O Lord: hide not thy face from us.

Cause us to hear thy loving kindness in the morning, for in thee do we trust.

Cause us to know the way wherein we should walk, for unto thee do we lift up our souls.

Teach us to do thy will, for thou art our God: thy spirit is good, lead us into the land of uprightness.

Quicken us, O Lord, for thy name's sake; for we are thy servants.

LIX.

MY soul cleaveth unto the dust: quicken thou me, O God, according to thy word.

I have declared my ways, and thou heardest me: teach me thy statutes.

Make me to understand the way of thy precepts; so shall I talk of thy wondrous works.

Remove from me the way of lying, and grant me thy law gracioufly.

I have chofen the way of truth; thy judgments have I laid before me.

I have ftuck unto thy teftimonies: O Lord, put me not to fhame.

I will run the way of thy commandments, when thou fhalt enlarge my heart.

LX.

THOU art my portion, O Lord: I have faid that I would keep thy words.

I entreated thy favour with my whole heart: be merciful unto me, according to thy word.

I thought on my ways, and turned my feet unto thy teftimonies.

I made hafte, and delayed not to keep thy commandments.

I am a companion of all them that fear thee, and of them that keep thy precepts.

The earth, O Lord, is full of thy mercy: teach me thy ftatutes.

LXI.

LXI.

For ever, O Lord, thy word is settled in heaven.

Thy faithfulness is unto all generations: thou hast established the earth, and it abideth.

The heavens continue this day according to thine ordinances; for all are thy servants.

I will never forget thy precepts, for with them thou hast quickened me.

I am thine, save me; for I have sought thy precepts.

Till I die I will not remove mine integrity from me.

My righteousness I hold fast, and will not let it go; my heart shall not reproach me so long as I live.

For what is the hope of the hypocrite, though he hath gained, when God taketh away his soul?

The triumphing of the wicked is short, and the joy of the hypocrite but for a moment.

But as for me, I will call upon the Lord; I will look up unto him who judgeth true judgment.

For behold, my witness is in heaven, and my record is on high.

LXII.

LET my cry come near before thee, O Lord: give me underſtanding according to thy word.

Let my ſupplication come before thee: deliver me according to thy word.

My lips ſhall utter praiſe, when thou haſt taught me thy ſtatutes.

What time I am afraid, I will hope in thee.

My tongue ſhall ſpeak of thy word; for all thy commandments are righteouſneſs.

Let thine hand help me; for I have choſen thy precepts.

I have longed for thy ſalvation, O Lord; and thy law is my delight.

Let my ſoul live, and it ſhall praiſe thee: and let thy judgments help me.

I have gone aſtray, like a loſt ſheep: ſeek thy ſervant, for I do not forget thy commandments.

LXIII.

RIGHTEOUS art thou, O Lord; and upright are thy judgments.

O how love I thy law, it is my meditation all the day.

Part II. PENITENCE, AND PRAYER.

The law of thy mouth is better to me than thousands of gold and silver.

Thy statutes have been my songs in the house of my pilgrimage.

I called them to remembrance in the night: I communed with mine own heart, and my spirit made diligent search.

The words of the Lord are pure words; as silver tried in a furnace of earth, and purified seven times.

I understand more than the antients, because I keep thy precepts.

I will refrain my feet from every evil way, that I may keep thy word.

I will never depart from thy judgments, for thou hast taught me.

How sweet are thy words unto my taste; yea, sweeter than honey to my mouth.

Through thy precepts I get understanding, therefore I hate every false way.

LXIV.

LORD, I have hoped for thy testimonies, and done thy commandments.

My soul hath kept thy testimonies, and I love them exceedingly.

Thy word is a lamp unto my feet; and a light unto my path.

I have sworn, and I will perform it, that I will keep thy righteous jndgments.

Accept, I beseech thee, the free-will offerings of my mouth, O Lord; and teach me thy law.

Thy testimonies have I taken as an heritage for ever, for they are the rejoicing of my heart.

I have inclined my heart to perform thy statutes always, even unto the end.

All my ways are before thee.

LXV.

THY testimonies, O Lord, are wonderful; therefore doth my soul keep them.

The entrance of thy words giveth light; it giveth understanding to the simple.

Thy testimonies are my delight, and my counsellors.

Open thou mine eyes, that I may behold wondrous things out of thy law.

Look thou upon me, and be gracious unto me, as thou usest to be unto those who love thy name.

Deal bountifully with thy servant, that I may live, and keep thy word.

Deliver

Deliver me from the oppression of man; so will I keep thy precepts.

Make thy face to shine upon thy servant; and teach me thy statutes.

Order my footsteps in thy word; and let not any iniquity have dominion over me.

LXVI.

BE merciful unto me, O God, be merciful unto me; for my soul trusteth in thee: yea, in the shadow of thy wings will I make my refuge.

I will always cry unto God most high; unto God, who performeth all things for me.

He shall send from heaven, and save me: my God shall send forth his mercy, and his truth.

Truly my soul waiteth upon God; from him cometh my salvation.

He only is my rock and my salvation; he is my defence, I shall not be greatly moved.

Trust in him at all times, ye people: pour out your heart before him; God is a refuge for us.

God hath spoken once, twice have I heard this, that power belongeth unto God.

Also unto thee, O God, belongeth mercy; for thou wilt render unto every man according to his works.

Surely

Surely men of low degree are vanity, and men of high degree are a lye; to be laid in the balance, they are altogether lighter than vanity.

But I will sing of thy power; yea, I will sing aloud of thy mercy in the morning: for thou hast been my defence, and my refuge.

Unto thee, O my strength, will I sing.

In God have I put my trust, I will not be afraid what man can do unto me.

Thou hast delivered my soul from death.

I will praise thee for ever, because thou hast blessed me; and I will wait on thy name, for it is good before thy saints.

LXVII.

HEAR my cry, O God, attend unto my prayer.

Be not thou far from me, O Lord: O my strength, haste thee to help me.

From the end of the earth will I cry unto thee, when my heart is overwhelmed: lead me to the rock that is higher than I.

Hear, O God, hear my vows: give me an heritage with those who fear thy name.

So will I sing praise unto thy name for ever, that I may daily perform my vows.

I will

I will abide in thy tabernacle for ever, I will truſt in the covert of thy wings.

I ſaid unto the Lord, Thou art my God, hear the voice of my ſupplications, O Lord.

I cried unto the Lord with my voice, and he heard me out of his holy hill.

I will praiſe thee; for thou haſt heard me, and art become my ſalvation.

The Lord hath heard my ſupplications; the Lord will receive my prayer.

I will declare thy name unto my brethren; in the midſt of the congregation will I praiſe thee.

My praiſe ſhall be of thee in the great congregation; I will pay my vows before them that fear him.

Thou art he that took me out of the womb; thou didſt make me hope when I was upon my mother's breaſt.

I laid me down, and ſlept; I awaked, for the Lord fuſtained me.

Thou art my hiding-place; thou ſhalt preſerve me from trouble, thou ſhalt compaſs me about with ſongs of deliverance.

I will freely ſacrifice unto thee: I will praiſe thy name, O Lord, for it is good.

Be of good courage, and he ſhall ſtrengthen your heart, all ye that hope in the Lord.

LXVIII.

LXVIII.

TEACH me, O Lord, the way of thy statutes, and I shall keep it unto the end.

Give me understanding, and I shall keep thy law; yea, I shall observe it with my whole heart.

Make me to go in the path of thy commandments, for therein do I delight.

Incline my heart unto thy testimonies, and not to covetousness.

Turn away mine eyes from beholding vanity, and quicken thou me in thy way.

Stablish thy word unto thy servant, who is devoted to thy fear.

Turn away my reproach, which I fear; for thy judgments are good.

Behold, I have longed after thy precepts; quicken me in thy righteousness.

LXIX.

HOW amiable are thy tabernacles, O Lord of hosts!

My soul longeth, yea, even fainteth for the courts of the Lord: my heart and my flesh crieth out for the living God.

Yea,

Yea, the sparrow hath found an house, and the swallow a nest for herself, where she may lay her young, even thine altars, O Lord of hosts, my King and my God.

Blessed are they that dwell in thy house: they will be still praising thee.

Blessed is the man whose strength is in thee.

O Lord God of Hosts, hear my prayer: give ear, O God, to my supplication.

Behold, O God, our shield, and look upon the face of thine anointed.

For a day in thy courts is better than a thousand: I had rather be a door-keeper in the house of my God, than to dwell in the tents of wickedness.

For the Lord God is a sun and a shield: the Lord will give grace and glory: no good thing will he withold from them that walk uprightly.

O Lord of hosts, blessed is the man that trusteth in thee.

LXX.

LET thy mercies come unto me, O Lord: even thy salvation, according to thy word.

So shall I have wherewith to answer him that reproacheth me; for I trust in thy word.

And take not the word of truth utterly out of my mouth, for I have hoped in thy judgments.

So shall I keep thy law continually for ever and ever.

And I will walk at liberty, for I seek thy precepts.

I will speak of thy testimonies also before kings, and will not be ashamed.

And I will delight myself in thy commandments, which I have loved.

My hands also will I lift up unto thee, and I will meditate in thy statutes.

LXXI.

GIVE ear to my words, O Lord, consider my meditation.

Hearken unto the voice of my cry, my King and my God: for unto thee will I pray.

My voice shalt thou hear in the morning, O Lord; in the morning will I direct my prayer unto thee, and will look up.

For thou art not a God that hath pleasure in wickedness: neither shall evil dwell with thee.

The foolish shall not stand in my sight: thou hatest all workers of iniquity.

Thou

Thou shalt destroy them that speak falshood: the Lord will abhor the bloody and deceitful man.

But as for me I will come into thy house in the multitude of thy mercy: and in thy fear will I worship toward thy holy temple.

Lead me, O Lord, in thy righteousness; make thy way strait before my face.

Let all those that put their trust in thee, rejoice: let them ever shout for joy; because thou defendest them: let them also that love thy name, be joyful in thee.

For thou, Lord, wilt bless the righteous; with favour wilt thou compass him as with a shield.

LXXII.

I Hate vain thoughts, O my God: but thy law do I love.

Thou art my hiding place, and my shield: I hope in thy word.

Depart from me, ye evil doers; for I will keep the commandments of my God.

Uphold me according to thy word, that I may live: and let me not be ashamed of my hope.

Hold thou me up, and I shall be safe: and I will have respect unto thy statutes continually.

Thou lovest righteousness and hatest wickedness.

Thou

Thou haſt trodden down all them that err from thy ſtatutes: for their words are falſehood.

Thou putteſt away all the wicked of the earth like droſs: therefore I love thy teſtimonies.

My fleſh trembleth, for fear of thee, and I am afraid of thy judgments.

LXXIII.

O GOD, thou art my God, early will I ſeek thee.

Evening and morning, and at noon, will I pray and cry aloud, and thou ſhalt hear my voice.

My ſoul thirſteth for thee, becauſe thy loving-kindneſs is better than life: my lips ſhall praiſe thee.

Examine me, O Lord, and prove me; try my reins, and my heart.

I will waſh my hands in innocency; ſo will I compaſs thine altar, O Lord.

My ſoul followeth hard after thee, thy right hand upholdeth me.

Lord, I have loved the habitation of thy houſe, and the place where thine honour dwelleth.

Becauſe thou haſt been my help, therefore in the ſhadow of thy wings will I rejoice.

That I may publiſh with the voice of thankſgiving, and talk of all thy wondrous works.

And

And I will blefs thy name while I live; I will lift up my hands in thy name.

The righteous fhall be glad in the Lord, and fhall truft in him; and all the upright in heart fhall glory.

LXXIV.

I CRIED with my whole heart, hear me, O Lord: I will keep thy ftatutes.

I cried unto thee, fave me, and I fhall keep thy teftimonies.

I prevented the dawning, and cried: I hoped in thy word.

Mine eyes prevented the night watches, that I might meditate in thy word.

Hear my voice, according unto thy kindnefs: O Lord, quicken me according to thy judgment.

Thou art near, O Lord; and all thy commandments are truth.

Concerning thy teftimonies, I have known of old, that thou haft founded them for ever.

I have feen an end of all perfection; but thy commandment is exceeding broad.

LXXV.

SURELY God will not do wickedly, neither will the Almighty pervert juftice.

For the work of a man fhall he render unto him, and caufe every man to find according to his ways.

Will he efteem thy riches? No, not gold, nor all the forces of ftrength.

He accepteth not the perfons of princes, nor regardeth the rich more than the poor; for they are all the works of his hands.

The cry of the poor cometh unto him, and he heareth the cry of the afflicted.

When he giveth quietnefs, who then can make trouble? and when he hideth his face, who then can behold him?

Behold, God is great, and we know him not; neither can the number of his years be fearched out.

Look unto the heavens, and fee; and behold the clouds, which are higher than thou.

If thou finneft, what doeft thou againft him? or if thy tranfgreffions be multiplied, what doeft thou unto him?

If thou be righteous, what giveft thou him; or what receiveth he of thy hand?

Thy wickedness may hurt a man, as thou art; and thy righteousness may profit the son of man.

Behold, O Lord, we are vile, what shall we answer thee? We will lay our hand upon our mouth.

LXXVI.

SURELY it is meet to be said unto God, I have borne chastisement, I will not offend any more.

We have sinned, with our fathers; we have committed iniquity, we have done wickedly.

There is none that doeth good; no, not one.

O God, thou knowest our foolishness, and our sins are not hid from thee.

How many are our iniquities, and our sins! Make us to know our transgressions.

Lord, we cry unto thee, make haste unto us; give ear unto our voice when we cry unto thee.

We abhor ourselves, and repent in dust and ashes.

Will the Lord cast off for ever? and will he be favourable no more?

Is his mercy clean gone for ever? doth his promise fail for evermore?

Hath God forgotten to be gracious? hath he in anger shut up his tender mercies?

Help us, O God of our falvation, for the glory of thy name; and deliver us, and purge away our fins, for thy name's fake.

O defpife not the work of thy hands.

Let our prayer come before thee; incline thine ear, and fave us.

O Lord God of hofts, how long wilt thou be angry againſt the prayer of thy people! we periſh at the rebuke of thy countenance.

Turn us again, O God, and cauſe thy face to ſhine, and we ſhall be faved.

And cleanſe us thoroughly from our guiltineſs, and waſh away our fins from before thy face; and vifit us with thy favour, even life everlaſting. Amen.

LXXVII.

BLESSED is he whoſe tranfgreffion is forgiven, whoſe fin is covered.

Blefſed is the man to whom the Lord imputeth not iniquity, and in whoſe ſpirit there is no guile.

We have finned, what ſhall we do unto thee, O thou preferver of men.

I acknowledged my fin unto thee, and mine iniquity have I not hid: I faid, I will confeſs mine iniquities unto the Lord, and thou forgaveſt the iniquity of my fin.

Sing

Sing unto the Lord, O ye faints of his; and give thanks at the remembrance of his holinefs.

For his anger continueth but a moment: in his favour is life: weeping may endure for a night, but joy cometh in the morning.

LXXVIII.

HAVE mercy upon me, O God, according to thy loving kindnefs: according to the multitude of thy tender mercies blot out my tranfgreffions.

Wafh me throughly from mine iniquities, and cleanfe me from my fin.

For I acknowledge my tranfgreffion; and my fin is ever before me.

Againft thee, thee only have I finned, and done evil in thy fight; that thou mighteft be juftified when thou fpeakeft, and be clear when thou judgeft.

Behold, thou defireft truth in the inward parts; and in the hidden part thou fhalt make me to know wifdom.

Make me to hear joy and gladnefs, that the bones which thou haft broken may rejoice.

Hide thy face from my fin, and blot out all mine iniquities.

Create in me a clean heart, O God; and renew a right spirit within me.

Cast me not away from thy presence; and take not thy holy spirit from me.

Restore unto me the joy of thy salvation; and uphold me with thy free spirit.

Then will I teach transgressors thy ways; and sinners shall be converted unto thee.

O Lord, open thou my lips, and my mouth shall shew forth thy praise.

For thou desirest not sacrifice, else would I give it: thou delightest not in burnt offerings.

The sacrifices of God are a broken spirit: a broken and a contrite heart, O God, thou wilt not despise.

LXXIX.

O LORD, rebuke us not in thine anger; neither chasten us in thy hot displeasure.

We have sinned, what shall we do unto thee, O thou Preserver of men.

Turn us, O God of our salvation; and cause thine anger towards us to cease.

Wilt thou be angry with us for ever? wilt thou draw out thine anger to all generations?

Wilt thou not revive us again, that thy people may rejoice in thee.

Shew us thy mercy, O Lord; and grant us thy salvation.

I will hear what God the Lord will speak; for he will speak peace unto his people, and to his saints: but let them not turn again to folly.

Surely his salvation is nigh unto them that fear him, that glory may dwell in our land,

Thou hast forgiven the iniquity of thy people; thou hast covered all their sin.

Mercy and truth are met together; righteousness and peace have kissed each other.

Truth shall spring out of the earth, and righteousness shall look down from heaven.

Yea, the Lord shall give that which is good; and our land shall yield her increase.

Righteousness shall go before him, and shall set us in the way of his steps.

LXXX.

UNTO thee, O Lord, do I lift up my soul.

O my God, I trust in thee, let me not be ashamed.

Yea, let none that wait on thee be ashamed; let them be ashamed who transgress without cause.

Shew me thy ways, O Lord; teach me thy paths.

Lead me in thy truth, and teach me: for thou art the God of my falvation; on thee do I wait all the day.

Remember, O Lord, thy tender mercies, and thy loving kindneſſes; for they have been ever of old.

Remember not the fins of my youth, nor my tranfgreſſions; according to thy mercies remember thou me, for thy goodneſs fake, O Lord.

Good and upright is the Lord; therefore will he teach finners in the way.

The meek will he guide in judgment; and the meek will he teach his way.

All the paths of the Lord are mercy and truth, unto fuch as keep his covenant and his teſtimonies.

For thy name's fake, O Lord, pardon mine iniquity; for it is great.

What man is he that feareth the Lord? him fhall he teach in the way which he fhall choofe.

His foul fhall dwell at eafe; and his feed fhall inherit the earth.

The fecret of the Lord is with them that fear him; and he will fhew them his covenant.

Mine eyes are ever toward the Lord; for he fhall pluck my feet out of the net.

Let

Part II. PENITENCE, AND PRAYER.

Let integrity and uprightnefs preferve me: for I wait on thee.

O keep my foul, and deliver me: let me not be afhamed, for in thee do I put my truft.

PART

PART III.

OCCASIONAL and PROPHETIC PSALMS.

I.

WHY do the heathen rage, and the people imagine a vain thing?
The kings of the earth set themselves, and the rulers take counsel together against the Lord, and against his anointed, saying,
Let us break their bands asunder, and cast away their cords from us.
He that sitteth in the heavens shall laugh; the Lord shall have them in derision.
Then

Then shall he speak unto them in his wrath, and vex them in his sore displeasure.

Yet have I set my King upon my holy hill of Zion.

I will declare the decree: the Lord hath said unto me, Thou art my son, this day have I begotten thee.

Ask of me, and I shall give thee the heathen for thine inheritance, and the uttermost parts of the earth for thy possession.

Thou shall break them with a rod of iron; thou shall dash them in pieces like a potter's vessel.

Be wise now therefore, O ye kings; be instructed, ye judges of the earth.

Serve the Lord with fear, and rejoice with trembling.

Kiss the Son, least he be angry, and ye perish from the way, when his wrath is kindled but a little.

Blessed are all they that put their trust in him.

II.

COMFORT ye, comfort ye my people, saith our God.

For he hath laid help upon one who is mighty, he hath exalted one chosen out of the people.

The

He hath made him also his first-born, higher than the kings of the earth.

He shall judge thy people with righteousness, and thy poor with judgment.

The mountains shall bring peace to the people, and the little hills by righteousness.

He shall judge the poor; he shall save the children of the needy, and shall break in pieces the oppressor.

They shall fear thee as long as the sun and moon endure, throughout all generations.

He shall come even like rain upon the mowen grass, as showers that water the earth.

In his days shall the righteous flourish; and abundance of peace, so long as the moon endureth.

He shall have dominion also from sea to sea, and from the river unto the ends of the earth.

They that dwell in the wilderness shall bow before him; and his enemies shall lick the dust.

The kings of Tarshish, and the isles, shall bring presents; the kings of Sheba, and Seba, shall offer gifts.

Yea, all kings shall fall down before him; all nations shall serve him.

For he shall deliver the needy when he crieth; the poor also, and he that hath no helper.

He shall spare the poor and needy, and shall save the souls of the needy.

He shall redeem their souls from deceit, and violence; and precious shall their blood be in his sight.

And he shall live, and to him shall be given of the gold of Sheba: prayer also shall be made for him continually, and daily shall he be praised.

There shall be an handful of corn in the earth upon the top of the mountains; the fruit thereof shall shake like Lebanon, and they of the city shall flourish like grass of the earth.

His name shall endure for ever: his name shall be continued as long as the sun: and men shall be blessed in him; all nations shall call him blessed.

Blessed be the Lord God, the God of Israel, who only doeth wondrous things.

And blessed be his glorious name for ever and ever; and let the whole earth be filled with his glory. Amen and Amen.

III.

THE Lord said unto my Lord, sit thou at my right hand, until I make thine enemies thy footstool.

The Lord shall send the rod of thy strength out of Zion: rule thou in the midst of thine enemies.

Thy people shall be willing in the day of thy power,

power, in the beauties of holiness: the dew of thy youth shall be more numerous than the dew-drops from the womb of the morning.

The Lord hath sworn, and will not repent, thou art a priest for ever after the order of Melchizedeck.

The Lord at thy right hand shall strike through kings in the day of his wrath.

He shall judge among the heathen, he shall fill the places with the dead bodies: he shall wound the heads over many countries.

He shall drink of the brook in the way: therefore shall he lift up the head.

IV.

GOD is our refuge and strength, a very present help in trouble.

Therefore will we not fear, though the earth be removed, and the mountains be carried into the midst of the sea.

Though the waters thereof roar, and be troubled, though the mountains shake with the swelling thereof.

There is a river, the streams whereof shall make glad the city of God: the holy place of the tabernacles of the most high.

God is in the midst of her; she shall not be moved: God shall help her, and that right early.

The heathen raged, the kingdoms were moved: he uttered his voice, the earth melted.

The Lord of hofts is with us; the God of Jacob is our refuge.

Come, behold the works of the Lord, what wonders he hath wrought in the earth.

He maketh wars to ceafe unto the end of the earth; he breaketh the bow, and cutteth the fpear in funder; he burneth the chariot in the fire.

Be ftill, and know that I am God: I will be exalted among the heathen, I will be exalted in the earth.

The Lord of hofts is with us; the God of Jacob is our refuge.

V.

IF it had not been the Lord, who was on our fide, now may Ifrael fay:

If it had not been the Lord, who was on our fide, when men rofe up againft us:

Then they had fwallowed us up quick, when their wrath was kindled againft us.

Then the waters had overwhelmed us, the ftream had gone over our foul.

Then the proud waters had gone over our foul.

Blefled be the Lord, who hath not given us a prey to their teeth.

Our

Our foul is efcaped as a bird out of the fnare of the fowlers; the fnare is broken, and we are efcaped.

Our help is in the name of the Lord, who made heaven and earth.

VI.

I LOVE the Lord, becaufe he hath heard my voice, and my fupplications.

Becaufe he hath inclined his ear unto me, therefore will I call upon him as long as I live.

Then called I upon the name of the Lord; O Lord, I befeech thee, deliver my foul.

Gracious is the Lord, and righteous; yea, our God is merciful.

The Lord preferveth the fimple: I was brought low, and he helped me.

Return unto thy reft, O my foul, for the Lord hath dealt bountifully with thee.

For thou haft delivered my foul from death, mine eyes from tears, and my feet from falling.

When my fpirit was overwhelmed within me, then thou kneweft my path.

I will walk before the Lord in the land of the living.

I believed, therefore have I fpoken: I was greatly afflicted.

What shall I render unto the Lord, for all his benefits towards me?

I will take the cup of salvation, and call upon the name of the Lord.

I will pay my vows unto the Lord, now in the presence of all his people.

Precious in the sight of the Lord, is the death of his saints.

O Lord, truly I am thy servant; I am thy servant, and the son of thine handmaid: thou hast loosed my bonds.

I will offer to thee the sacrifice of thanksgiving, and will call upon the name of the Lord.

I will pay my vows unto the Lord, now in the presence of all his people.

In the courts of the Lord's house, in the midst of thee, O temple of the Lord.

Praise ye the Lord.

VII.

NOT unto us, O Lord, not unto us, but unto thy name give glory, for thy mercy, and for thy truth's sake.

Wherefore should the nations say, Where is now their God?

But our God is in the heavens; he hath done whatsoever he pleased.

Their

Their idols are silver and gold, the work of men's hands.

They have mouths, but they speak not; eyes have they, but they see not.

They have ears, but they hear not; noses have they, but they smell not.

They have hands, but they handle not; feet have they, but they walk not; neither speak they through their throat.

They that make them are like unto them, so is every one that trusteth in them.

O Israel, trust thou in the Lord: he is thy help and thy shield.

O house of his people, trust in the Lord: he is thy help and thy shield.

The Lord hath been mindful of us, he will bless us.

He will bless them that fear the Lord, both small and great.

The Lord shall increase you more and more, you and your children.

You are blessed of the Lord, who made heaven and earth.

The heaven, even the heavens are the Lord's; but the earth hath he given to the children of men.

The dead praise not the Lord; neither any that go down into silence.

But we will bleſs the Lord, from this time forth and for evermore. Praiſe ye the Lord.

VIII.

LORD, make me to know mine end, and the meaſure of my days what it is, that I may know how frail I am.

Behold, thou haſt made my days as an hand's-breadth, and mine age is as nothing before thee: verily, every man at his beſt eſtate is altogether vanity.

Surely every man walketh in a vain ſhew; ſurely he is diſquieted in vain: he heapeth up riches, and knoweth not who ſhall gather them.

When thou with rebukes doſt correct man for iniquity, thou makeſt his beauty to conſume away like a moth.

Surely every man is vanity.

Our days are ſwifter than a weaver's ſhuttle: the eye of him that hath ſeen us ſhall ſee us no more: thine eyes are upon us, and we are not.

As the cloud is conſumed, and vaniſheth away; ſo he that goeth down to the grave ſhall come up no more.

He ſhall not return again to his houſe, neither ſhall his place know him any more.

Thou prevaileſt for ever againſt him, and he paſſeth ;

paſſeth; thou changeſt his countenance, and ſendeſt him away.

His ſons come to honour, and he knoweth it not; and they are brought low, but he perceiveth it not of them.

Remove thy ſtroke away from us, we are conſumed by the weight of thy hand.

O enter not into judgment with thy ſervants, for in thy ſight ſhall no man living be juſtified.

But we have truſted in thy mercy, our heart ſhall rejoice in thy ſalvation.

We ſhall behold thy face in righteouſneſs; we ſhall be ſatisfied when we awake in thy likeneſs.

And now, Lord, what wait I for? my hope is in thee.

I was dumb, I opened not my mouth, becauſe thou didſt it.

Hear my prayer, O Lord, and give ear unto my cry: hold not thy peace at my tears; for I am a ſtranger with thee, and a ſojourner, as all my fathers were.

O ſpare me, that I may recover ſtrength before I go hence, and be no more.

IX.

AS the hart panteth after the water-brooks; ſo panteth my ſoul after thee, O God.

My soul thirsteth for God, for the living God; when shall I come, and appear before his presence?

How long wilt thou forget me, O Lord? For ever? How long wilt thou hide thy face from me?

Consider and hear me, O Lord my God; lighten my eyes, ere I sleep the sleep of death.

I will say unto God, My rock, why hast thou forgotten me? Thou art the hope of my life, why dost thou cast me off?

O send out thy light and thy truth; let them lead me, let them bring me unto thy holy hill, and to thy tabernacles.

Then will I go unto the altar of salvation, unto God my exceeding joy; yea, upon the harp will I praise thee, O God my strength.

And the Lord will command his loving kindness in the day-time; and in the night his song shall be with me, and my prayer to the fountain of my life.

Why art thou cast down, O my soul? and why art thou disquieted within me? Hope thou in God; for I shall yet praise him, who is the health of my countenance, and my God.

X.

X.

LORD, thou haft been our dwelling-place through all generations.

Before the mountains were brought forth, or ever thou hadft formed the earth and the world, from everlafting to everlafting thou art God.

Thou turneft man to deftruction, and fayeft, Return, ye children of men.

For a thoufand years in thy fight, are but as yefterday when it is paft, and as a watch in the night.

Thou carrieft them away as with a flood, they are afleep: in the morning they are like grafs which groweth up.

In the morning it flourifheth, and groweth up. In the evening it is cut down, and withereth.

We fpend our years as a tale that is told.

What man is he that liveth, and fhall not die? Shall he deliver his foul from the hand of the grave?

Thou haft fet our iniquities before thee, our fecret fins in the light of thy countenance.

The days of our years are threefcore years and ten: and if by reafon of ftrength they be fourfcore years, yet is their ftrength labour and forrow; for it is foon cut off, and we fly away.

So teach us to number our days, that we may apply our hearts unto wisdom.

XI.

THIS is the day which the Lord hath made; we will rejoice and be glad therein.

I was glad when they said unto me, Let us go into the house of the Lord.

Open to me the gates of righteousness; I will go into them, and I will praise the Lord.

This is the gate of the Lord, into which the righteous shall enter.

Our feet shall stand within thy courts, O Zion.

Peace be within thy walls, and prosperity within thy palaces.

Let thy priests be clothed with righteousness, and let thy saints shout for joy.

For our brethren and companions sake we will now say, Peace be within thee.

Blessed be he that cometh in the name of the Lord; we have blessed you out of the house of the Lord.

Save now, we beseech thee, O Lord: O Lord, we beseech thee send now prosperity.

Let our prayer be set before thee as incense, and the lifting up of our hands as the evening sacrifice.

Thou art good, and doſt good: teach us thy ſtatutes.

XII.

MAN that is born of a woman is of few days, and full of trouble.

He cometh forth like a flower, and is cut down: he fleeth alſo as a ſhadow, and continueth not.

Although affliction cometh not forth out of the duſt, neither doth trouble ſpring out of the ground:

Yet man is born to trouble as the ſparks fly upwards.

His days are determined: the number of his months are with thee: thou haſt appointed his bounds that he cannot paſs.

For there is hope of a tree, if it be cut down, that it will ſprout again, and that the tender branch thereof will not ceaſe.

Though the root thereof wax old in the earth, and the ſtock thereof die in the ground:

Yet through the ſcent of water it will bud, and bring forth boughs like a plant.

But man dieth, and waſteth away; yea, man giveth up the ghoſt, and where is he?

As the waters fail from the ſea; as the flood decayeth, and drieth up:

So man lieth down, and riſeth not again, till the

the heavens be no more: they shall not awake, nor be raised out of their sleep.

XIII.

WE have heard with our ears, O God; our fathers have told us what work thou didst in their days, in the times of old.

We will not hide them from our children; shewing to the generation to come, the praises of the Lord, and his strength, and his wonderful works that he hath done.

That the generation to come may know them, even the children that shall be born; that they may set their hope in God, and not forget the works of God, but keep his commandments.

For they trusted not in the bow; neither did the sword save them:

Neither did their own arm save them; but thy right hand and thine arm, and the light of thy countenance, because thou hadst a favour unto them.

For thou didst save them from their enemies, and didst put those to shame that hated them.

God is known in our palaces for a refuge.

Surely the wrath of man shall praise; the remainder of wrath shalt thou restrain.

Remember us, O Lord, with the favour that
thou

thou bearest unto thy people: O visit us with thy salvation.

Give us help in trouble; for vain is the help of man.

That we may see the good of thy chosen, that we may glory with thine inheritance.

We would seek unto God, and unto God would we commit our cause.

God is the judge; he pulleth down one, and setteth up another.

Save us, O Lord our God, to give thanks unto thy holy name, and to triumph in thy praise.

Arise for our help, and redeem us for thy mercy's sake.

So we thy people, and sheep of thy pasture, will give thee thanks for ever; we will shew forth thy praise to all generations.

XIV.

IS there not a set time to man upon earth? Are not his days also like the days of an hireling?

All flesh shall perish together, and man shall turn again unto dust.

One dieth in his full strength, being wholly at ease and quiet.

Another dieth in the bitterness of his soul, and never eateth with pleasure.

They shall lie down alike in the dust, and the worms shall cover them.

Our years pass away; our purposes are broken off, even the thoughts of our heart.

We are but of yesterday, and know nothing, because our days upon earth are a shadow.

Our days also are few; and we go whence we shall not return, to the land of darkness and the shadow of death.

There the wicked cease from troubling, and the weary are at rest.

There the prisoners rest together, they hear not the voice of the oppressor.

The small and great are there, and the servant is free from his master.

Shall we receive good at the hands of the Lord, and shall we not receive evil?

All the days of my appointed time will I wait, till my change cometh.

Naked came I out of my mother's womb, and naked shall I return thither.

The Lord gave, and the Lord hath taken away, blessed be the name of the Lord.

XV.

XV.

THE Lord is my rock and my salvation, my strength, and the lifter up of mine head: though he slay me, yet will I trust in him.

For I know that my Redeemer liveth, and that he shall stand at the latter day upon the earth.

And though after my skin worms destroy this body, yet in my flesh shall I see God.

Whom I shall see for myself; and mine eyes shall behold, and not another, though my reins be consumed within me.

The days of man's years are few; they are consumed like smoke: he lieth down among the clods of the valley, he passeth away, he is seen no more.

But thou shalt quicken us again, and bring us up again from the depths of the earth.

What time I am afraid, I will trust in thee.

He that is our God, is the God of salvation; and unto the Lord belong the issues from death.

MORAL PSALM

OMITTED.

THE Lord is in his holy temple: the Lord's throne is in heaven; his eyes behold, his eye-lids try the children of men.

God judgeth the righteous, and God is angry with the wicked every day.

If he turn not, he will whet his fword; he hath bent his bow, and made it ready.

He hath alfo prepared for him the inftruments of death; he ordaineth his arrows againft the perfecutors.

O let the wickednefs of the wicked come to an end, but eftablifh the juft; for thou, the righteous Lord, trieft the heart and the reins.

The Lord trieth the righteous; but the wicked, and him that loveth violence, his foul hateth.

Upon the wicked he fhall rain fnares, fire and brimftone, and an horrible tempeft; this fhall be the portion of their cup.

But

MORAL PSALM.

But the righteous Lord loveth righteousness, his countenance doth behold the upright.

I will praise the Lord according to his righteousness, and will sing praise unto the Lord most high.

The Lord shall judge the people.

THE END.

www.ingramcontent.com/pod-product-compliance
Lightning Source LLC
Chambersburg PA
CBHW030819190426
43197CB00036B/598